MIDLIFE IRISH

MIDLIFE IRISH

~ *Discovering My Family and Myself* ~

FRANK GANNON

WARNER BOOKS

An AOL Time Warner Company

Copyright© 2003 by Frank Gannon
All rights reserved.

Warner Books, Inc., 1271 Avenue of the Americas, New York, NY 10020

Visit our Web site at www.twbookmark.com.

An AOL Time Warner Company

Printed in the United States of America
First Printing: February 2003
10 9 8 7 6 5 4 3 2 1

The Library of Congress Cataloging-in-Publication Data

Gannon, Frank.
   Midlife Irish : discovering my family and myself / Frank Gannon.
      p. cm.
   ISBN 0-446-52678-9
   1. Ireland—Description and travel. 2. Ireland—Social life and customs.
3. Gannon, Frank—Journeys—Ireland. 4. Irish Americans—Biography.
5. Gannon, Frank—Family. I. Title.

DA978.2.G36 2003
305.891'62078'092—dc21
[B]
                                              2002033104

Book design by Giorgetta Bell McRee

For my sister Mary and her parents

Acknowledgments

I'd like to thank David Greene, a great dining companion and a great genealogist. I'd also like to thank Dennis Shue, Jr., who read the manuscript when it was a big stack of poorly Xeroxed pages. Thanks also to the fine Irishman John Aherne for a great job. Also thanks to Rob McMahon, who helped me a great deal before he embarked. Much thanks to Scott Waxman, who helped me with the birth of this. Much thanks to Bob Castillo and Sean Delvin, who did a great job. May the road rise to meet all these people, whatever that means. Finally, I'd like to thank my children, Aimee, Anne, and Frank, and my wife, Paulette, for making my time on the planet brilliant.

Contents

∾ On the Beach ∾

I am six years old. I am sitting on the beach in Ocean City, New Jersey. My brother and sister are in the water. My mom and dad are sitting on the beach chairs behind me. We have an umbrella that my dad rented, and Mom and Dad are doing what they usually do at the beach. They are sitting still. It is a perfect cloudless day in the middle of July.

I am using a plastic device with a spring-loaded plunger to make "bricks" out of wet sand. I am building something. I don't know what it's going to be. My mom asks my dad something. I remember this conversation very well.

"You miss it?" My mom had her serious look.

"No, I don't," my dad answered. He didn't have to think about it. "Do you?"

"Sometimes," said Mom. "You *never* miss it?"

Again, he didn't have to think at all. "Never," he said.

I didn't understand what they were talking about. When I looked at them, they were staring straight out at the ocean.

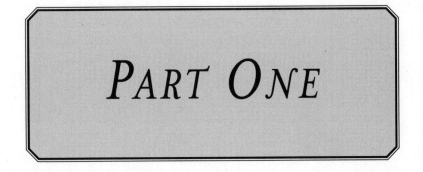

PART ONE

ONE

~ *Icebergs* ~

I'm a middle-age guy, if I'm going to live another forty-nine years. I know this isn't going to happen. There's nothing "middle" about this. If I get the same deal as my dad, I am left with sixteen years. I'm a three-quarters-age guy, which is a more accurate word than "middle."

I live in Demorest, a little town in the mountains of northern Georgia. There are about seven hundred other people who also live here. I think I know most of them. I would say that Demorest is like Mayberry on that Andy Griffith show, but Mayberry appears to be a much more complex place.

The most famous person ever born in Demorest is Johnny Mize, the Hall of Fame baseball player. He was born here, played for the Giants, the Cardinals, and the Yankees. Then he came back to Demorest and died. When I first moved here, there was a sign, "Demorest, home of Johnny Mize." They took the sign down when he died.

I am a married man with three kids. My full name is Francis Xavier Gannon. Like almost everybody named "Francis Xavier," I'm Irish.

I've never thought much about that.

My mom was born in Anne Forde in Ballyhaunis, a little town in the West of Ireland, County Mayo. My dad, Bernard Gannon, grew up on a farm near the city of Athlone near the center of Ireland. They came over to America long before I was born. They didn't know each other in Ireland, but by the time I was born, they had known each other almost twenty years.

My parents were pretty old when they started a family. World War II started right after they got engaged, so they had a long engagement. Knowing my dad, I think they probably would have had a long engagement without the war.

My mom was born in 1908, my dad four months later. They came to America for many reasons. The main reason was money. They became American citizens. They never seriously considered going back to Ireland. My father did go back to the Old Country, for two weeks in 1968, when he knew he had cancer. My mom may have visited Ireland again when she was young, but during my life, she only went back that one time with my dad.

By the time I came around, Dad owned his own little business, a workingman's bar. So if they had wanted, they could easily have afforded to go back. My dad never mentioned going back, and my mom never mentioned it when he was around. After she knew about the cancer she mentioned going back a lot.

My parents weren't that interested in Ireland, at least as far as I could tell. They never discussed "the troubles" or anything else that was happening on the island. I never heard them mention anyone they knew who had stayed in Ireland. The people back there were history for them, history they didn't want to hear about.

The category "Irish people in America," however, was a subject of extreme interest in the Gannon house. When they saw anyone on television who had "gotten off the boat," they had to discuss just how Irish the guy still was. Someone like Bing Crosby was vaguely Irish. He talked American. You would have to know about his "people" to nail him as Irish. Someone like the singers Carmel Quinn and Dennis Day, people just off the boat, still sounded Irish. Crosby was better because he was more American.

There was some debate just how Irish the off-the-boat

talkers were. Although they spoke with a brogue, my father suspected them of "putting it on." He had a very good ear for someone pretending to be more Irish than thou. Sometimes when Dennis Day or Carmel Quinn talked, my dad would close his eyes and shake his giant head. To pretend that you talked with a brogue when you really were Americanized was a truly appalling practice. Sometimes my dad would have to leave the room after they said something "Irish" that smelled of phoniness. My mom was more tolerant than my dad, but she also hated "pseudo-Irish." She just wasn't as demonstrative as Dad.

My parents had a thick brogue. My sister Mary, my brother Bud, and I sound more like a standard television announcer than someone who's "Irish." My dad liked this. My mom had no comment, but she didn't seem to think it was bad that her children sounded American. Once I pretended I had an English accent, and they really didn't like it, so I stopped.

It is, of course, impossible to totally break one's "language ties." I remember a dialect specialist in college who told me exactly where I was born, where I grew up, and where my parents came from. It was as if I had a sign on my forehead to the dialect specialist, but to the general public I was "disguised."

My dad actually tried to get rid of his brogue, but saw it was hopeless and abandoned the project. My mom never tried. Her speaking voice was as west Irish as the rocks on the coast of Mayo. I can close my eyes and listen to her funny/sad Irish voice any time I want to.

I do have one ability I seem to have inherited. I can tell if an actor is accurate in his Irish accent. If the actor is a little off on his feigned Irishness, I can tell. Brad Pitt had the most egregiously wrong "Irish accent" in the quickly forgotten *The Devil's Own* ("I'm not goin' bahk!") as an IRA guy in America with a hidden past. I react to his voice in that film like I react to the sound of a balloon being rubbed with wet hands.

A few actors do an Irish accent, to my ear, very accurately. I guess Liam Neeson doesn't count, but Julia Roberts, to me, can sound as if she just got off the boat. Johnny Depp (*Chocolate*) and Robin Wright (*The Playboys*) also receive high grades for Irish verisimilitude. Tom Cruise (*Far and Away*): accent B minus, performance D.

My dad had a dilemma that he had to deal with every day. He didn't want to be identified as Irish, yet every time he spoke, he gave himself away. Therefore, he didn't talk unless he couldn't get out of it. Talk only as a last resort.

My dad was a pretty mysterious guy. When I was little, I thought maybe he was Batman. He tended to conceal certain details, when the details weren't to his liking. One lifelong, very weird thing my dad did was lie about his birthday. He didn't lie about the year, which would have been understandable. He lied about the date he was born.

Dad's birthday, he always told us, was August 25. I discovered that he was lying, after he died. He was really born on December 21. My nephew's birthday is on that date, so you would think it would slip. But no, he was born in August, and that was it. He kept up this minor lie his whole life.

When he died, and I saw "December 21, 1908" on his birth certificate, I was startled. Why, I thought, would he lie about such a ridiculous thing? He wanted to be another astrological sign? After my dad's funeral, I asked my dad's brother, John Gannon, who was as gregarious as my dad was quiet, why my dad misrepresented his birthday.

"He didn't want to be younger than his wife," he said quickly, as if that explained things. For the Gannon brothers.

My dad spoke about his life back in Ireland as little as possible. The only subject he spoke less about was sex—or perhaps "sex" and "life back in Ireland" were tied for last. My mom, who talked all the time about almost everything, rarely mentioned her childhood. My mom was the easiest person in the world to talk to. She would chat about *everything*. Things that you didn't think *had* great detail, she would discuss in great detail, but about life back in the Old Country, she was almost as silent as my dad.

If I did ask them about Ireland, which I did often when I was in college, my mom would steer the subject away from Ireland, while my dad would do his imitation of a rock. Because my mom kept talking, I felt I had a chance of getting something about the Old Sod, but no dice. If you talked to her for twenty minutes, you would have taken a huge conversational walk. You might talk about baseball and God and whatever, but I very rarely got her to talk about her childhood.

The Indian who answers, "How" to every question was a blabbermouth compared to my dad. Once, riding in the car, I tried the direct approach. "What was it like when you were in school?"

"Different," he said, and that was it.

Growing up, I knew that I was Irish in much the same way I knew that I had asthma. I knew I had it but I didn't know anything about it. Unlike asthma, however, I would never grow out of being Irish. What little I did know about my parents' early life I had to piece together from tiny overheard pieces of conversations and a few inferences. I was a kid, and I wasn't a great inferer, but I did gather a few facts:

- Although my parents are almost exactly the same age and Ireland is a very small country, they did not know each other until they were in America.
- My dad arrived in America first, but my mom became a citizen before he did. They were both in their twenties when they became official Americans. (They were, of course, also official citizens of Ireland until the day they died.)
- Mom and Dad knew that they were leaving Ireland permanently. In this they were like most Irish people. For

Irish immigrants coming to America, Ireland is the country of the past. Irish people are the least likely immigrants to return to their native country. Depression-era Philadelphia, for my parents, was still better than what they left behind. Frank McCourt's mom and dad, who returned to Ireland, are an exceptional case. (With Ireland's bright economy, this is probably going to change soon.)

- My parents had a very long courtship. They met; they dated; they got engaged. My dad, who was desperate for a job, decided to enlist in the army. He hated it. When his hitch was almost up, World War II started. He wound up spending ten years in the army. He got out, they got married. They were both almost forty.

- Mom and Dad didn't say what their time in Ireland was like, but they did train me to suspect anything that was pseudo-Irish. I am happy they never lived to see *Leprechaun in the Hood*.

My parents' one and only trip to Ireland was something that my dad strongly resisted. He needed a lot of coaxing. I remember long conversations featuring my mom on the "Pro-Ireland" side and my dad on the "Con-Irish." These started without warning. Sometimes something came on television that suggested Ireland, and crossfire would begin. Sometimes it was something overtly Irish. More often it was something subtle. In the right mood, merely the sight of the color green was enough to set it off.

Look at that on television.

Yeah.

Those hills look like round stone.

They don't.

Yes they do. Exactly.

It's just television. It's nothing.

Let's go.

I can't.

Why?

I can't leave the place.

Frank and Jack can handle it. Look at him. He's all grown up.

I can't do it. And that's it.

Come on.

My dad would turn to me with a desperate look. Then he'd take off his glasses and rub his eyes. Then he would say, "She won't stop."

There were many hours of this but they finally went. The hardest thing for my dad was leaving the bar, which he never called anything except "The Place." He worried about his bar all the time. He was sure that no one could run it the right way.

But he finally agreed, and they went back to Ireland for a couple of weeks. After he said he would go if she would just stop talking about it, my mom whispered something in my ear.

"He just needed coaxing." Five thousand hours of coaxing.

I also needed coaxing.

A lot of Americans saw the miserable, poverty-stricken youth of Frank McCourt as representative of the typical first-generation Irish experience. I got public sympathy that I hadn't earned in social situations. I was introduced to a woman in her twenties at a party of some sort. I said hello. Then my friend, by way of introduction, said, "His parents were born in Ireland." My friend could have said many other things. She might have said, "He needs the plot explained to him after he sees Agatha Christie movies." She might have said, "The poor bastard voted for Ralph Nader." But she picked the Irish thing. The person I was introduced to suddenly looked sympathetic.

"I'm so sorry," she said.

I will take whatever sympathy is offered, but there is nothing in my childhood that would normally evoke pity. In this I'm like most first-generation Irish-Americans. The overwhelming majority had experiences like mine. Their parents were generally very poor, but America was a new start. In America they worked hard, stayed married, and tried hard to raise their kids. There were no drunken beatings and no starvation. Christmas was always nice. The only drunk people I saw weren't related to me. The Gannon kids grew up to be more American than Irish. They had a little neurosis here and there, but nothing a little Prozac wouldn't fix.

So it wasn't really that surprising that my parents left the past in the past. However, no one ever successfully cuts himself off from his own past, and, as J. M. Barrie said, "Nothing much matters after you're six years old."

I came in near the end of my parents' lives. I completely missed the beginning, so I'm going back to the theater.

Of my two parents, my dad was by far the more mysterious. Except for her Irish past, I was very close to my mom, but I really didn't even know much about my dad's *post*-Ireland life. My dad was over forty when I was born, so by the time I started to get curious about his past, he was already around sixty. We didn't talk very much. When he died, at sixty-five, I was still waiting to have a good talk.

I would spend about two hours alone with my dad every week, so it seems remarkable that we had very little communication. However, my dad talked in a very distinctive, non-revelatory way. I can say, after "talking" with him for several hundred hours, I still didn't know any more about him. He wanted it that way. Let me explain.

Every Sunday we would ride to the bar to clean up. My dad liked to thoroughly clean the place on Sunday, the only day of the week he closed. It was against the law in New Jersey to sell take-out liquor, beer, or wine then, so it probably wouldn't have been a big profit day, but my dad said that Sunday was a special day, set aside for church and family, and closing was the right thing to do. My dad closed the bar on Sundays, Good Friday, New Year's Day, and Christmas. The Good Friday closing used to seriously puzzle winos. They would knock on the door, peer through the glass, and scratch their heads in wonderment. It can't be Sunday already, thought the winos. Why is this bar closed today?

I know this because my dad and I drove past the bar on Good Fridays, and I could see the winos lost in wonderment outside. There was another, open bar three blocks away, but this was *their* bar, and they were genuinely perplexed.

"They're heathens," my dad said.

There was no work on Good Friday, but every Sunday morning it was clean-up time. We'd get up around 6:00 A.M., go to mass, get some breakfast, and head over to the bar. My dad liked to get a fanatical right-wing preacher on the radio and listen to him while he worked. His favorite right-wing preacher was named Carl McIntire, who would just spout off. He hated Catholics and Irish people, but he really hated Irish Catholic people. My dad would listen to McIntire say something horrible about Irish Catholics, and it did something very few other things could do: It made him laugh.

I would have preferred that we turn on some rock 'n' roll. Even some Robert Goulet would be better than McIntire.

"This is my place," he said. "When you get your own place you don't have to listen to McIntire. You can listen to your own crap." That was the end of that.

My father's conversation during our work resembled *Bartlett's Familiar Quotations*. He never said (I think), "Beauty is Truth; Truth Beauty." But he tended to develop certain responses, and once he had a response that pleased him, he stayed with it.

These were his observations. I recorded them for posterity.

Sometimes something would have happened in my life, and I was perplexed by it. This would cause me all kinds of heartache because I was a teenager beset by life's difficulties. When I expressed this to my dad, he always eloquently said the same thing:

> *What could have happened happened.*
> *—Bernard Gannon*

Sometimes while laboring over a mop or one of the inadequate tools that had to do for this epic undertaking, I might be overcome with lethargy. I would take a big gulp of air and let it out, shaking my head and showing great weariness at my impossible task. Surely, he would not ask an animal to work like this. Where is the humanity? At these times my dad would say:

> *Hard work isn't easy, isn't it?*
> *—Bernard Gannon*

My dad would retain his Bartlett's quality even after we finished work and drove home. It was just a mood he got into on Sundays. I remember this scene. My dad is in the living room watching TV. I am in the backyard playing one-on-one basketball with one of my friends. I was very tough to beat on my home court because I knew all the cracks in the pavement in our driveway. After playing, and inevitably triumphing, I, along with my vanquished friend, would be very thirsty. When I was about seventeen, my dad let me steal a beer or two on Sundays, if I asked. You had to ask permission. I would say something like, "Is it okay if _____ and I get a couple of beers?" His reply was:

> *What are we, Chinamen?*
> *—Bernard Gannon*

Thirty years later, I still do not fully understand this question, but I remember it, as if it were the Pledge of Allegiance to the Flag.

When I went to Ireland I knew it would not be easy, but I was going to find out at least something about this man.

TWO

∽ *Irish DNA* ↝

I know a lot about "Ireland."

It's extremely green there. It's green everywhere. In the winter, it's still green. Just green and more green. There are about seventy-five shades of green. Whenever anybody wants to remind themselves that they're Irish, they say, "It's time for the wearin' of the green." It's green city.

That's pretty much it as far as the landscape goes. There are also the Irish people.

There are young men there and old men there. The young men are often called "brawny." They wear little hats and will, if provoked, punch you in the mouth. The old men are smaller than the young men. The old men smoke pipes and make mysterious, gnomic pronouncements and statements about things. The statements sound like questions. Instead of saying, "Nice night," they say, "Are you after havin' dinner, is it?"

Everybody says, "Top of the mornin'." No one knows what this means.

There is a lot of punching in "Ireland." The old men are not as quick to punch you in the mouth, but they will, if sufficiently provoked, give it to you. You'll be standing there with your hand on your bleeding mouth. Then they'll say, "Are you after bein' punched in the mouth, is it?"

Both the old men and the young men drink too much. Way too much. They call this "after havin' a drop taken."

Everyone in Ireland is continually looking for some excuse to drink. When somebody dies, they really drink a lot. They drink something called "poteen." The entire nation needs to be after checking in the Betty Ford Clinic, is it? But nobody ever does. Alcohol is funny. Everybody laughs about it. A drunken Irishman is very funny.

No one ever suffers from drinking. They just "sleep it off" and everything is fine again.

All the drinking causes a lot of that fiddle music, which is played, continuously, like Musak, all across the land. If there were a volcano in Ireland, they would be playing that music while it erupted and killed thousands. Many would die dancing.

Even though everyone in Ireland can dance, they cannot dance and move their upper body at the same time. Irish people like to get in giant Rockettes-style lines and dance like crazy while their upper bodies remain stationary.

The Irish women come in two varieties: young and old. The young ones look very good, and most of them have red hair. You call them either "Colleens" or "Lassies." I, personally, would not call them "Lassies" because of the connection to the TV show. I would call them "Colleens." After I got to know them, I would call then "Darlin' Colleens."

The Colleens are often described as "headstrong." The platonic ideal of an Irish girl looks like Maureen O'Hara. They look great but if you look at them right in the eye, they smile for a second and turn their face.

That is darlin'.

When the Irish women get older, they go to church a lot, and many people refer to them as "saintly." They are never far from rosary beads. When some Irish guy dies, no matter how bad that guy is, they can, and do, say of him, "At least he loved his mother."

Everybody in Ireland is Catholic. If you are born and grow up, and, for some reason, do not completely and utterly accept the Catholic dogma in its entirety, then you have to leave. The other Irish people will watch your plane or boat leave and say, "We won't be missin' him." Or they may say, "We won't be missin' the likes of him."

But they will. They will write songs about him leaving. The songs will have pipes in them. Someone, somewhere in the song will be referred to as "darlin'."

The priests and the nuns of Ireland form a large part of the population. Almost everyone has a priest or a nun in their family. The priests, when they are young, tend to resemble the young Bing Crosby. When they get older, they turn into Barry Fitzgerald. All priests are extremely good at all sports. They are particularly adept in boxing. If you "put on the gloves" with an Irish priest, watch out because he will beat the crap out of you. An old Irish priest always has a photograph of himself taken when he was young. He will be in trunks and gloves and will be the one-time welterweight champion of Sligo or something, a title he abandoned when he became a priest.

You don't mess with Irish priests. They would call them bad mother_____, but they don't use that kind of language over there.

If an Irish man isn't a priest he can be a cop or a bartender or a farmer. There are no other professions available.

Irish policemen are "tough but fair." When they are described, those exact words are used. There are no Irish policewomen. If an Irish woman is interested in keeping the general order, she becomes a nun.

Irish nuns are also startlingly good at sports. An Irish nun will always strike out a kid who thinks he's a wise guy. Irish priests can play baseball, basketball, and football extremely well, even though they will always play with those big black robes on. And if you act like a wise ass they will humiliate you. But they'll still love you.

Irish people are all happy-go-lucky. They say "sure and begorrah" a lot, and like "top of the morning" no one ever knows what it means. They are extremely lucky. If you read about the history of Ireland, "lucky" is the last adjective that would seem to describe it. But everybody says, "The Luck of the Irish," so there must be something to it. No one says "The Bad Luck of the Irish," which seems a lot more appropriate.

That is Ireland, a place I am very familiar with. The place I am familiar with, however, exists only in advertisements for cereals and soap, and in certain movies now largely owned by Ted Turner who is owned by AOL Time Warner. The real Ireland, I couldn't tell you. My mom and dad were, of course, born in Ireland. Their mom and dad were born there too. And so on and so on, back into what science-fiction movies call "the mists of time." But I woke up one day and realized that I really didn't know who I was. I was an Irish guy, but that was all I really knew about Ireland.

I'm an American. I like American stuff. I like the Philadelphia Phillies. Every year I can name their lineup. I start every morning from April to September checking the box scores. I know all the characters on *Gilligan's Island*.

I grew up in Camden, New Jersey. If you have never been there, I will describe it as "Philadelphia's exciting sister city to the east." I took Latin and German in college and high school, but American English is the only language I will ever really know, the only language I will ever dream in. I know two things in Gaelic: "Erin go bragh" and "poga ma hough." One means "Ireland forever" and the other means "kiss my ass." I once got a book on Gaelic, looked at it, and put it away. As Steve Martin said of the French, they have different words for *everything*.

But there was always something "Irish" floating around in the atmosphere at my house on Forty-ninth Street. My friends, when they met my mom and dad, would always say something like, "Wow, your parents are really Irish." Or, "They're like from Ireland, huh?" Or, among some, "They talk funny, huh?"

My mom had little holy water fonts beside the doorways

in my house, and I got used to "blessing myself" (dipping a finger in the font and making the sign of the cross whenever I entered a room) at a very early age. There were crucifixes in every room in my house except the bathroom, and I am not completely sure there weren't any in there. There was an Infant of Prague, a little statue of the Christ Child, which my mom would dress in different ways according to the church calendar, sitting on the radiator cover in our living room. There were also religious pictures all over the house, and my family would, without fail, dutifully kneel and say the rosary every night before bed.

We would also stop at the appointed hours and say the Angelus prayer. There was a print of that famous Millet painting *The Angelus* in our living room, the only "objet d'art" in the house.

My house had so much religious stuff that Paul Gartland, my friend, saw the movie *Hunchback of Notre Dame* on television and then told people that criminals often ran into my living room, fell to their knees, and screamed, "Sanctuary!"

My mom and dad both listened to the *Irish Hour* on the radio (it always seemed to be on, making me suspect it was longer than an hour), and my dad always read the Irish newspapers, even though he never mentioned "back there." They were members of the Hibernians, and on Saint Patrick's Day *and* the day after Saint Patrick's Day, we got to stay home from school. My dad's bar was called GANNON'S IRISH AMERICAN REFRESHMENT PARLOR.

There were two framed pictures in my dad's bar, one on each side of the front door. One was Franklin Delano Roosevelt, and the other was Jesus Christ. Sometimes my dad would point them out to people and assume a vaguely threatening posture that seemed to say, "Any questions?"

My dad had a little accordion-thing with buttons on one side. When he played it, with his enormous, alarmingly scarred fingers, it always sounded like the same song. I began to think of it as "The Irish Song." I looked in his songbook.

There were several different songs in there. I can't remember the names, but they had titles like, "Maggie in the Bushes," and "Bringin' in the Rot," and that old favorite, "Down by the Side of the Ditch." They all sounded like the same song played at slightly different speeds. By the time I was thirteen, I was really sick of "The Irish Song." Even today, if you say "Deedly deedly dee" in my presence I get a little nauseated.

Eventually I drew additional conclusions about my parents' past in Ireland: These were "additional supplementary information."

1. It was very tough, and they had no money.

My dad would occasionally say something like, "You don't know how easy you have it." I didn't know any details about the early life of my mom and dad, but my dad did have a very peculiar attitude toward nature that, I believe, had its origin back there in the Old Country. When I was a kid, I asked him if I could have a dog. He looked at me as if I had just asked him for something really unspeakable. The way he said no made me think he was saying, "I have had enough of animals in my house."

2. They lived on farms, but it wasn't like the farm life on Lassie.

My dad was not one with nature.

One time, when I was about ten, I saw a hand-painted sign, "Tomato Plants for sale." I knocked on the door and an old guy with a baseball hat answered the door. He was very friendly. He showed me his tomato plants. He had hundreds of them. I bought four of them and took them home. I dutifully planted them in my backyard. I watered them and looked at them proudly. I didn't particularly like tomatoes, but I was very much looking forward to watching them grow into big round red beauties. I thought of it as a science/ nature experiment. When I was little, I loved "mad scientists." I used to lock the bathroom door and pour every liquid I could find into the sink. I wanted to see if something weird would happen like it did in the movies whenever anybody mixed stuff together. Nothing ever happened except I occasionally stained the sink.

But I enjoyed my tomato plants. They changed a little every day. "The Tomato that Attacked . . ." movie hadn't yet been made, or I would have thought of it while I watched my plants.

The next evening, my dad was mowing the lawn with his big green Sears power mower. He was just about finished when he saw something new over by the back fence—my tomato plants. He got a peculiar look, halfway between disgust and shock. Then he went over and mowed them down—my tomato plants. Then he went back over them a few times to make sure they were really gone. Then, just to make *really* sure, he mowed them down one more time.

I looked at my plants. There was nothing left but . . . tomato plants that had been run over by a lawn mower three times. This sight made me start crying. The brutality of the man. I ran into the house and buried my face in my pillow. My mom came in and asked what was going on. I told her what had happened. She was not shocked. She said that was just the way Dad was.

Later, my dad explained himself. We are not farmers. We do not grow things. We do not live on a farm. We are better than that.

Any questions?

3. People who say how great Ireland is, and how beautiful it is, don't know anything about Ireland.

My dad told me this, in different words, approximately ten thousand times. "Ah, you don't know what it was like, Fransie." He said that to me a lot when I was little. I wondered why he couldn't get my name straight. Every time he "had a little talk" with me, he called me "Fransie."

But even when he called me Fransie, he really didn't tell me much about Ireland. All I knew was that farms are really bad. All crops should be mowed down.

I decided to find out about Ireland.

*   *   *

First I had to really think: What did I think "Irish" was, and how did I form my impressions?

I thought back.

I was in third grade when the teacher, Miss Burke, asked if anybody was "third generation." I had no idea what this meant, and I could see that most of the other kids didn't either. Miss Burke explained.

Almost everybody in America, except the Indians, came from somewhere else. If your parents came from somewhere else, you were "first generation." If your grandparents came from somewhere else, you were "second generation." And so forth.

It turned out that I was the only kid who was "first generation."

Miss Burke said, "And we don't have to ask what country they came from, do we?"

Why not? I thought. At recess I asked her.

"I didn't have to ask, Frank," she said, "because *the map of Ireland is all over your face.*"

This was, I thought, puzzling. I looked at my face. Pretty normal. I wasn't the most perceptive kid in the world. I got most of my knowledge from looking at movies. That summer I got the idea of what an Irish person was from watching movies.

An Irish person is just like a cowboy. I figured this out by watching John Ford movies.

John Ford is widely supposed to have characteristically introduced himself, "I'm John Ford. I make westerns." He might have said, "I created what people in America think when they hear the word 'Irishman.'"

Ford specialized in the movie genre "western." For this he used John Wayne. But he also used Henry Fonda, Victor Mature, Ward Bond, Walter Brennan, and, as they say, "a host of others."

It seemed to me odd, when I first discovered it, that John

Ford was an Irish guy. When I was a kid, I was surrounded by Irish people, and, because the Walt Whitman Theater was four blocks from my house, I was also, if you consider fifties American television and movies, pretty close to surrounded by westerns.

When I was a kid I would watch a movie that would be classified as a "western" almost every week. My absolute oldest television memory is of watching (half watching—I must have been four years old) an anthology series that featured old westerns. My mom told me that one of the first names I ever spoke was "Johnny Mack Brown." She would do an impression of me saying it: "Johnny Mack Bwown! Johnny Mack Bwown!" This would cause me acute embarrassment in high school, but I got over it.

Johnny Mack Brown, certified cowboy movie star, was one of the recurring actors on the particular anthology show that I watched with my mom and my brother and sister. My mom told me later that, at the end of the show, she would ask me, my sister, and my brother, "Who is your favorite cowboy?" Mary and Bud had varying answers, but I would always answer "Johnny Mack Bwown!" I was, she told me later, just about screaming.

Johnny Mack Brown. Those four syllables are all that remains in my memory banks of that particular cowboy. I know that I said, "Johnny Mack Bwown" when asked the cowboy question. I have absolutely no idea who he is or what he looks like. I could not pick him out of a lineup.

Years later, I was going to look up "Johnny Mack Brown" and attach a face to the syllables, but I didn't. It seemed purer to leave him as the only person I "know" only as a sound.

So, although I could have bumped into Johnny Mack Brown at an airport and not known it, he is real, to me, only as a sound. I do know that Johnny Mack Brown rode a horse and had a six-gun and wore one style of those hats. That's about it.

Like "Johnny Mack Brown," the concepts "Irish" and "western" were never quite clear in my young mind.

Even now, described in a certain manner, *The Quiet Man* sounds just like one of Ford's westerns. There is an outsider who is a nice guy but, when aroused, capable of violence, something he's really good at. There is a beautiful untamed landscape with a breathtaking, beautiful heroine, and there is, of course, the bad guy. The bad guy is also violent, but not as good at violence as the good guy is.

This good guy is a man of few words. He's tall, and he is John Wayne, aka Marion Morrison. The first time we see him, he's getting off a train. The voice we hear is the voice of his dead Irish mother:

Don't you remember it, Seannie, and how it was? The road led up past the chapel and it wound and it wound. And there is the field where Dan Tobin's bullock chased you. It was a lovely house, Seannie, and the roses, well your father used to tease me about them, but he was that fond of them too.

Wayne's name is Sean Thornton. Ford had relatives named Thornton, and he liked to say that he was born "Sean." The movie has a family feel to it. Ford's brother Francis and his son-in-law Ken Curtis were in the cast, which is packed with Ford's "regulars." They were doing what they usually did for John Ford—making a western.

If you watch *My Darling Clementine* and follow it with *The Quiet Man,* there is no mistaking it. Those cowboys were really Micks with bigger hats.

THREE

⌁ *Green Simians Within* ⌁

In writing this book, I read a lot about the Irish coming to America. American history isn't the prettiest story in the world, but Ireland's role in American history is, at the beginning, a particularly ugly chapter. The theme is basically "Who gets to oppress whom this year?" Irish immigrants start out oppressed, then swiftly become the oppressor.

The eighteenth century was the first Irish immigration to America. The first wave was Protestant. They settled in the South. Like most immigrant groups, they were stereotyped (period drawings show the newly arrived Irish largely as a form of drunken monkey-men with porkpie hats and pipes in their mouths).

The next wave, the famine immigrants, was much larger. Period representations, drawings for newspapers, still emphasized the hats, the pipes, and the booze, but the monkeys seem to have gotten much more violent. These monkeys aren't comic. They're still funny looking, but they're threatening, especially when they are drunk, and they are drunk all the time. America seems scared of these monkeys. One of the sons of these Irish people became the baddest man on the planet (circa 1880s), so maybe the drawings aren't that fanciful.

This wave was, of course, largely Catholic. The first group of green monkeys (who had now morphed into southern gentleman planters and a few northern businessmen) actually tried to suppress the second green-monkey group. They largely failed. By the pre–Civil War era, it's too late to suppress that second Irish group anymore. They are by now almost human.

In 2002 America you still find that little green monkey-man once in a while, but he's usually confined to cereal boxes and Hallmark "humorous" Saint Patrick's Day greeting cards, and he's comic, not threatening. The truth is we're just not that scary anymore. Even his kids are not threatened by Gerry Cooney.

It is very possible to be a first-generation Irish-American in 2002 America and be almost completely divorced from Ireland, a country that, until recently, made divorce against the law. I am a walking example. I can go (except for brief flashes near the middle of March) an entire year without having a single "Irish moment." Nevertheless, the fatal Irish identity was still buried somewhere in my subconscious mind. One summer day a few years ago, it bobbed to the surface.

My "trigger" was rather unexpected, but, as my mom would say, there you go.

I was looking at a car with a mouth when I first decided to go to Ireland. It was a moment of, for me, deep meditation.

I was alone. I had just mowed the lawn. Whenever I mow the lawn I have "distant thoughts" because I don't like to think about mowing the lawn. I went inside and took a shower. The television, the great meditative tool, was on. It was a show (I think it was PBS) about "low riders," cars that are adapted to ride very slow, "bounce," and look cool. The show features many of these cars and their owners. One car had Pez dispensers, filled with Pez, glued all over. Maybe two hundred Pez dispensers. This got my attention.

The owner of the car told the interviewer that this car "made him look friendly. Especially to girls."

There was a low rider whose headlights had been turned into eyes. There were eyelashes and everything. There was a big nose on the hood. The best part, though, was the tongue. When the driver popped the hood latch, a big red tongue came out. "It made people laugh," said the owner. The car was painted a deep metallic green.

When the owner popped the hood, the unseen narrator said, "They see this as a part of their native culture."

That was my Jungian synchronicity Irish moment.

A green car with eyes and a mouth and a purple car with Pez dispensers. Native culture.

I began to think about my native culture. I grew up in New Jersey, so my native culture, to some, isn't that great a culture. Bruce Springsteen is probably the first thing you think of when you say "New Jersey." In 1984 I remember Ronald Reagan saying that his administration was deeply committed to that culture. Ronald Reagan said that during his re-election campaign. I remember thinking at the time that it was the most bullshit thing ever said by a politician.

Springsteen's songs are about fast cars and Jersey girls and the Jersey shore, and, of course, the always-popular "broken dreams." I remember when they almost made "Born to Run" the official state poem. A state senator objected to "Baby this town rips the bones from your back, it's a death trap, it's a suicide rap" as bad for tourism.

Native culture. I have eight Bruce Springsteen albums, but for me the Paragon of New Jerseyism is Frank Sinatra. His songs are about women and broken dreams, but there are no cars (except the elegiac honking limousine horn in "September of My Years").

If you want to tell something about a person's culture, it is usually informative to examine his living area. In *Do the Right Thing* Danny Aiello's pizza parlor "Wall of Fame" was given its proper cultural significance. The fact that there was not a single African-American on the wall was a telling anthropological pointer.

In my office, New Jersey is well represented. There is a framed letter I received from Frank Sinatra in a prominent position on my personal wall of fame. Sinatra sent me it thanking me for ridiculing Kitty Kelley (an apparent Irish woman) in a magazine article. I also have a framed copy of the Philadelphia Phillies 1964 roster and a Phillies button from 1980, the only year they were ever champions.

But the only Irish thing is an old sign that says "Help Wanted. No Irish Need Apply." Every Irish-American has the same sign. It's required.

In my albums it's the same story: forty-five Sinatras, eight Springsteens, two Chieftains, and that terrible "the Irish Tenors" CD.

I began to feel more inadequate than I normally feel. Every year of my youth, when my family went to the Hibernian Saint Patrick's Day Party I had heard one Irish guy ask another Irish guy this question. This was always followed by obscenities, so even then I knew it was not a good thing to be asked.

"What kind of Irishman are you?"

What kind of Irishman was I? I could hear a voice: "You wouldn't put a patch on an Irishman's ass!" I knew what kind of Irishman I was. I wear green on Saint Patrick's Day, that's what kind of Irishman I am.

This started to bother me. I was two-thirds through my life and I hadn't even been to Ireland once. I had never even kept up with my Irish relatives. I barely kept up with my Irish relatives in America. The idea of dying before I even bothered to see where I was from was a sad, sad thing.

So I watched the green car with the eyes and the mouth and I thought about Ireland. I wouldn't put a patch on an Irishman's ass. I didn't know what that meant, but it bothered me.

It is an often-made observation that there are more Irish people in America than in Ireland. Because of this, there are a lot of people like me, Irish people whose idea of Ireland is based on something that has no basis in reality. The authentic reality is the result of many sad circumstances—the potato famine, the English, the Irish economy, the English, and so on. But this situation has created a huge market for stuff that is directed at the "Irish Diaspora," Irish people who know nothing about Ireland, but feel a little guilty about it once in a while.

I feel a little sympathy toward these people because I'm one of them. It's very strange to consider: all these Irish people with a substitute country. But as with most things in the modern world, there is no "solution." Ireland is a tiny island, which is relatively sparse in population. If the population of the "Irish Diaspora" were all sent to Ireland, the entire island would be as tightly packed as New Jersey. If there were enough guys like me, it might turn into Jersey. Then what would we do?

All these people need their absent Ireland, and they get infusions of it on a regular basis. The highbrow Diaspora gets a never-ending stream of books that connect Ireland with everything in America. Ireland and Walt Whitman. Ireland and Thoreau. Ireland and Joseph Campbell. The mythic area here is a particularly rich lode, and the racks of Barnes and Noble are filled with examinations of Oisin's wanderings and Queen Maeve's thoughts. Plus wind chimes.

The longing for the Old Country has, in America, taken on a New Age aspect that is disturbing. It is responsible for the marketing of an appalling array of Celtic spiritualism that takes the form of "Celtic" CDs, meditation guides, and God knows what. This is a regrettable phenomenon, but at least it is (sort of) Irish in nature. In a group as large as Irish America, there has to be a huge number of Windham Hill fanciers.

Those guys are the Irish-Americans who have been to college. IQ-challenged members of the Diaspora (God knows there is no shortage) have their marshmallow-flecked cereal, their oddly blue soap, and, most important, their many, many varieties of alcohol. (It's all alcohol, but hey, I've seen people in Wildwood, New Jersey, argue about the merits of Bushmills versus Jamesons as if they actually *tasted* it before they swallowed.)

All these people also, of course, have to get back to Ireland and comb through it for whatever threads are to be found. Ireland right now is covered with every variety of American root-seeker. I know a *fifth*-generation dentist who has just returned from such a journey. He must have truly awesome genealogical abilities.

Irish America magazine is a thriving (and very well done) bimonthly periodical aimed at just this massive audience. You would think that a magazine that comes out six times a year and has, as its sole focus, Irish people in America would run out of things to say, but that is emphatically not the case. Irish America is larger than most countries, and *Irish America* is, in 2001, an extremely healthy publication.

Irish America, in all its numbers, is an enormously powerful cultural and economic force, but this has not always been the case, and that fact has a permanent position in the Celto-American (a new one!) cranial cavity. We used to be those monkeys, remember that? How can you forget? Here's a "No Irish Need Apply" sign. Put it in your den.

As has been often noted, this whole phenomenon has more to do with power of *numbers* than anything else. Twenty-first-century Irish America likes to say, like Stephen Crane's MAN, "Sir, I exist!" I have a lot of money and it's time that everybody notices me. Okay, you're noticed. Here's a magazine. You want anything else? Plane tickets?

Although there have been a lot of Irish in America for centuries, much of Irish America's past has been spent as a minor bit player in the movie of America. "Laborers and servants," however numerous, don't get to be the stars of the movie. There is no *Irish Stable Boy* magazine.

Today, however, Irish America contains leaders of industry and the arts. Has the monkey-man vanished? He is rare, but he can still be seen. Mister 2002 Irish-American need only walk through any greeting card display in March and see the same little green guy sitting on a rack, who says to him as he passes, "You are *still* a mick. Get used to it."

At this point this Irish-American man's green-man-group message doesn't bother him much. He doesn't write any letters or call any congressmen. He's above the fray now. His reaction is A, Doesn't notice, or B, Mild bemusement.

He walks out of the drugstore to get into his fine Japanese automobile and drives to an Italian restaurant with his Swedish girlfriend. His arrogance is well-grounded, this one. He knows certain facts that cannot be taken from him: In 1960 a monkey was elected president of these United States. When he turns on his high-definition television he sees the simian Peter Lynch walking in the rarefied air of big money, of cubic American Benjamins. What is he? Third generation?

The Irish-American has a sip of his Jamesons and thinks of where he is in the American structure, and he concludes that he's not anywhere near the basement. He thinks, *Am I to weep over a pig? The dog barks but the caravan goes on. I am a complex, well-paid human being. Need I concern myself with some little green monkey grinning at me on a rack at Walgreen's?*

But we like it here. Most Irish people who have come to America stayed here. I think, if everything were the same except that my parents had gotten rich in America, they still would have stayed in America. Irish people get along well with America. There are a variety of reasons for this. Many Irish people never even had the option of returning home, of course, but I don't think that there was, even for a second, a "get some dough and return to the Old Country" thing working in my parents' brains.

We speak the language, after all. A lot of first-generation Irish people made a huge social leap in one generation. Peasant to vice president in one generation. But now is a very good time to be an Irish guy in America because 2002 America is "being buried in Irish shit," as an acute (at that moment) Irish-American friend put it.

This is, I guess the American Celtic revival. The first one, the one over there with W. B. Yeats and Lady Gregory, was a whole lot lower on the bullshit scale, but this is, after all, America.

It's all bullshit, but we gotta have it. The Chieftains have gone the way of Shirley MacLaine/Riverdance. Where they once made beautiful versions of ancient Irish songs on ancient Irish instruments, they now have achieved great spiritual authenticity and their recent records are largely only played to force suspects to confess.

But who is this audience? Who buys this shit?

Yes, the woeful people in America with Irish-sounding last names. For some of us Ireland is a mythic land of Tir Nan Og with Michael Flately dancing on the shore while some chick named Moira sings like Joni Mitchell on nitrous oxide.

The real reason that the Irish in America (no matter how remote) have a bottomless appetite for this crap may be this: The most basic thing about being Irish isn't any of the things we often associate with it. It isn't a great sense of humor or a great talent for tragedy. It's the fact that Ireland is the most spiritual place on earth, and the major legacy that Irish people have always, in one form or another, left to their children is a deep abiding faith in God.

In America, of course, that's really not much of a possibility. So Irish people like to fill up the space with Ossian and Moira's divination keening followed by a large dose of dancers in those long lines.

When there is a hole you try to fill it. The spiritual hole in the middle of Irish America contains a whole lot of Celtic Moods CDs.

But for those Irish-Americans who just can't take "Yanni Plays the Druids," there is, of course, the thing itself. The eastern half of Ireland may be turning into America, but the western half is, in a lot of ways, the same place my parents left. Go back there, or go *back* to there, and, my son, you don't need any Celtic moods. You can go to the damn Catholic church and get your mood there, I can hear Dad say.

If my mom and dad were to have a look at *me* these days, they would approve of a lot of things. Three kids, two cars, big house. If they could look beyond the surface, however, they would see that I am a profound disappointment. My parents always told me that the most important thing in the world is what they call "the faith." When they discussed what an Irish person bequeaths to his children, they would say something like, "He didn't have much money at the end but he gave them the faith." And other Irish people would nod in assent.

My mom and dad had a faith. But somewhere in America, I misplaced it. I still go to church on Sunday and the authorities do not want me, but I just don't make it in spiritual land. I read a lot of philosophers in college and I decided that I was in Nietzsche land, but I have slowly stumbled over to what I would call "Bad Catholic Land."

There are many bad Catholics in America. They can go along with about 80 percent of what the Catholic Church says, but they disagree (sometimes violently) with the last 20 percent.

Bad Catholics think that homosexuals aren't sinning when they have sex. Bad Catholics think a woman has the right to decide what happens to her body. Bad Catholics aren't thrilled when the pope goes into a third-world developing country, a place where a great number of children die of starvation, and says that almost every form of birth control is morally wrong.

Finally, the most salient feature of Bad Catholics is their belief that even though they don't agree with everything the Catholic Church says, they still aren't going to quit. They are

going to stick around, keep pretty quiet, and be Bad
Catholics.

I grew up in America and became a Bad Catholic. I don't
have a rich spiritual life. My mom and dad, who grew up in
Ireland, did. I am now going to Ireland and I hope that I will
see just where I missed the boat.

FOUR

∽ *The Epic Journey* ∾

Like certain Italian wines, I have never traveled well. This may be because of experiences I had when I was young.

Our vacation when I was a kid consisted of the following: We lived right next to Philadelphia, on the Delaware River in New Jersey, and we would drive sixty miles to the Jersey shore and stay for two weeks in a rented house at Ocean City, the home, I later found out, of Gay Talese, but in those days beloved for its three challenging miniature golf courses on the boardwalk and the fact that there were no bars or even places to buy alcoholic beverages. Ocean City was "The Family Place amid the Sodoms and Gomorrahs of the Jersey shore."

Sixty miles, tops. This was not the Oregon Trail. But my dad made a major production out of this. To "avoid traffic," he would wake us up at 5:00 A.M. the day of the drive. My brother, my sister, and I would stumble out to the car clutching our pillows, and we would drive down to the shore. My sister and brother always fell asleep. I stared out the dew-laden window of my dad's '61 Dodge.

There were no cars on the road at that hour, just the occasional truck. Some of them would blink their lights. I never knew what that meant, but my dad seemed to think it was ominous. He would knit his brow, stare harder at the empty Route 9. Sometimes he would mutter the name of God.

Because I was young and because of the early hour—the

jolt of being taken from a warm bed and placed in a cold Dodge at 5:00 A.M.—I always thought that it was like my favorite show, the one my mother rarely let me see, *The Twilight Zone.* The episode where Burgess Meredith woke up and the world was dead.

There were still people in New Jersey driving down to the shore at 5:00 A.M. But they seemed *altered.* A single truck with a grim little Edward Hopper man peeking above the steering wheel. A solitary ominous walking black bird. One old lady crossing the road and turning her head in slow motion as we approached. I saw all this while the sun slowly crept up over the New Jersey shore horizon.

It was beautiful when we got there. After that grueling hour, sixty minutes on the road and now, Thank God! Thank God we had gotten up early enough to "beat the traffic"! We would get to our destination, Ocean City, around 6:30 A.M.

My dad would roll down the window. Smell that, you sleeping ones! Smell that!

I rolled down my window. Yes, the sea. I will always love that smell.

Then we would be going over bridges and my brother and sister would wake up. Look! A seagull! I don't think that I have ever been happier than when we rolled into Ocean City after our epic journey.

There was the house. It was always the same house. When I was four, on my first trip, I despaired when I saw it. I asked my mother in anguish, "Why did we sell our nice house and buy this crummy house?" By the time I was five I got the idea.

I loved the house, the weirdness of it. The sheets on the bed. The backyard with the strange gnarled tree. The little store up at the corner.

After we got there, it was, of course, still very early. We would wander around saying things like, "What time is it?" and taking short naps on the couch or the beds. Until finally, after what seemed like an eternity, it was time to go to the beach.

My dad loved this plan.

"Beats the cursed traffic," he would say.

At that point I know that I accepted the truth of this:

A big epic journey takes an hour. At the end, you are still in New Jersey.

I remember thinking once, on a Sunday drive with my dad, that Hershey, Pennsylvania, was "the wilderness." I remember him stopping the Dodge to go in and take a leak, and I remember getting out of the car to stretch my little legs. And I remember looking around and thinking, "Wow, this is like on Davey Crockett." Wilderness.

But now I was going to Ireland. Get on the plane. And when I got off, I wouldn't even be in New Jersey.

I sat at my kitchen table and went over this with Paulette, my wife, a woman I have spent virtually my entire adult life with. She has been to bizarre places, so it wasn't the traveling that was the bother. With her, it was the realization that she was going to have to be a character in a book.

"You have to be a character in this book because you are traveling with me and sharing my exciting and diverse Irish experiences while I write this gripping and moving saga." I didn't say exactly that, but pretty close.

Paulette said, "No, I do not want to be a character."

I said, "Why not?"

She said, "I am a very private person, and I do not want to be a 'character.'"

I was, to be honest, a little put out by her prima donna stunt. When you've been in the same room with a person while that person is going to the bathroom and you have had sex with that person and children with that person, I feel the term "private person" is no longer a usable term. I told her that I would be entirely truthful and would not say anything about her that she didn't want me to say unless it was really necessary or I wanted to get back at her in some way.

"I don't want you slandering me." She actually said that. That's a direct quotation.

I said that I would not legally slander her to the best of my knowledge of the definition of "slander," as I, a person who did not go to law school, understood it.

We arrived at a mutually satisfactory agreement without the aid of lawyers. I agreed that I would let her read the book before it was published and, if there was anything in there about her that she did not like, I would feel really bad about it and sympathize with her. At least that's the way I understood it. Nobody signed anything.

Ken, our friend, drove us to the airport. Ken is a lawyer, but the subject was never broached on our ninety-minute drive from Demorest to the Atlanta airport. Even though Paulette was now in the presence of a lawyer, she did not bring up the alleged "slander" issue. I take this as an implied agreement on her part.

We were soon parking at the vast, sprawling Atlanta Hartsfield Airport. If anything deserves the words "vast and sprawling," it's the Atlanta Airport. Also "irritating."

I hate airports, and Atlanta's is the most loathsome of all airports. I walked through the vast sprawling place and had grim thoughts. We decided to go to one of the bars in the airport, an idea I was very much in favor of.

We all had drinks and sat there without saying anything. Airports almost always make me feel bad. I trace my dread of airports to early systematic conditioning. Airports and hospitals are the places where everything bad happens. Or at least, in my experience, the last (and therefore permanent) memory of the really horrible bad things in life is formed there.

In truth I was a little frightened about what I might find over there in Ireland. My mom and dad's aversion to talking about Ireland might have, it occurred to me, some single horrifying reality. I could see my dad saying, "I've never told you this. But your great-grandfather was Titus Andronicus."

What I'm really worried about, I realize, is what I might

find out about myself. That is always the most horrifying thing to discover: that "the horror" lives right inside your own chromosomes.

Murderers and horse thieves are romantic figures until you know that you are permanently genetically hooked up to them. But there was another thread that had deeply bothered me in a very quiet but consistent way. It can be described in two words: "Irish Coldness."

The Cold Irish are not all Irish, but we recognize each other by our awkward, stuttering movement whenever some emotional display is appropriate. We do many things, but one trait is dominant. We do not touch other human beings unless absolutely necessary.

I have been aware of this quality in myself for many years, and I have tried (vainly) to overcome it. When I was in high school all of my friends were Italian and I would marvel at the ease with which they hugged and kissed and nuzzled each other. The way the men would kiss each other.

In my family the men did not even kiss women (often, even when they were married to them).

So I have, since youth, tried consciously to overcome the "Cold Irish" quality that is buried deep within my DNA.

I try to hug, but it's clumsy, artificial, forced, awkward, and Lurchlike. Sometimes I stumble over and try to hug people and I catch, over their shoulders, a look of utter, naked horror on their faces and I know one thing.

YOU, Frank Gannon, are a Cold Irish person. You should never touch another human being. You have tried, and have failed.

But, maybe, I think, Ireland is the key to all this. Maybe when I get over there I will, among my people, lose that surrounded-by-invisible-bodyguards quality.

Maybe once I am over there under Celtic sky, I will stand in the Celtic heather (whatever that is) and be transformed into an actual human being with three dimensions and at least three real authentic emotions. I will become a warmer, more Walton's Mountain person. I will just jump up and hug somebody. I will find out that I am deeper than I thought I was. To touch, not Indians, but Irish people. People like me. My blood. My brothers and sisters. I need to dance about madly when the fit is on me. Need to hug the girl down by the garden gate and shake hands with all my neighbors.

If you go to a travel agent, or watch airline commercials, or read travel magazines, you get the feeling that the Golden Age of Irish Tourism is here. I think Ireland is very hot now, as Australia was in the by-gone "Shrimp-on-the-Barbie" days. I picked up *USA Today* one day and I saw, on the front of one of their sections, a picture of a guy outside Dublin. I didn't know him, but something in his face was very familiar to me. It was a face I had seen on many heads at many Hibernian dinners. He was, as they say, pure mick. He looked like he should have had a cloth hat on his mick head and a pipe in his mick mouth. He looked as if he should be leaning on his rake out there in the bog fields.

But there is no bog, no rake. He has a yellow tie and an Armani suit and a cell phone and he is leaning against his BMW and the expression on his face says, "What I am talking about you can never understand." He has, finally, a really well-shined pair of black shoes. His shoes glimmer like onyx in the moonshine.

He is an Irish yuppie, two words that do not seem as if they can be next to each other.

I am not sure what I'm going to find over there. But it is too late to stop now. They call our row and I must show that woman my boarding pass to the land of saints and scholars and yuppies and, I hope, elves.

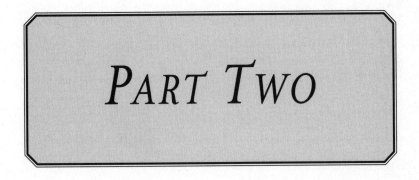

PART TWO

FIVE

~ *The Promised Land* ~

If this film of my parents' life were rewound, the part that I am now seeking, the pre-America part, would begin with their boat ride to Ellis Island. The end of my parents' Irish life would have been the day they got off the boat in America.

I was able to determine that they did come over on a boat, but when I tried to determine which boat, I ran into big trouble. They just didn't keep very good records of such things. Ellis Island is in the process of establishing a huge database that will eventually be able to tell everyone in America exactly when and how their ancestors got here. However, it's not finished yet. (Now it is, I believe—April 30, 2001.)

I spent many hours trying to establish my parents' boat, then, after finding nothing, I looked into the type of boat they came over on. I was able to narrow it down a little. I'm sure they didn't come over on a Carnival Cruise, but I was very curious about what their voyage was like. If I did write a moving account about their epic journey to America I'd be expanding beyond what I knew. What I know is, "It was bad." I'll have to omit the gripping story. It was better than *Mutiny on the Bounty* and worse than the first part of *Titanic* (the film).

I can, however, tell you about my trip *back* to Ireland. Although it wasn't even a boat ride it was, in its way, a nightmarish, near-death ride of survival. It was a trip of great horror that tested the souls of my fellow travelers and me.

We flew coach on Delta. I sat in a seat designed for a member of the United States Female Gymnastic Team. We were given a little plastic tray with poorly prepared food, and if we wanted alcoholic beverages, we had to pay for them.

But the final testament of man's cruelty to his fellow man was this: The in-flight movie was *Baby Geniuses*.

Lesser men wouldn't have made it, but somehow the human spirit finds ways to survive. We landed in Shannon Airport and every single person on that plane of evil survived. If Neil Diamond had been on that plane (in coach) he would have written something at least as good as "We're Coming to America." "We're Leaving America and We're Uncomfortable."

We knew that our adventure in Ireland would be a two-parter. We knew that our real mission was to find out about my mom and dad. The other part was just to check out Ireland.

As we walked off the plane we noticed that it was just about but not quite raining. After a week or so we realized that in Ireland it is almost always just about but not quite raining.

Shannon Airport looks as if it belongs in an old movie. It is markedly different from the standard American airport. The signs are of the "Eat at Joe's" variety and the luggage machine makes a loud clicking noise as it makes its bumpy way. The bathrooms look circa 1940. The men's-room urinal is one big metal trough where the men walk up, do their business, and depart. It looks like the urinal they usually have in prison movies.

When we got our luggage we were both pretty sore from siting in the Nadia seats for twelve hours, but we were excited because we were in Ireland. I felt very close to something, but I didn't know what it was. I couldn't wait to get over to the car rental.

In Ireland, for all the otherworldliness, they are a lot more sensitive to the realities of the environment. In America the mere sight of a guy in his SUV seems to scream out, "Screw all you Greenpeace pinko huggers of trees! I deny your existence!" In Ireland gas costs a lot, and the cars tend to be tiny. When I met Irish people with big cars they told me, without my asking, why they had to have a big car. If they had a big car, it was usually related to their livelihood or their family.

Gasoline is sold in liters, which seems to underline the sense that oil is not to be taken for granted. In America I never thought about "environmentalism," but in Ireland I was very conscious of it, and the amazing natural beauty of Ireland always reminded me.

We rented a Punta, a car not sold in America. If they did have it for sale in America people would laugh at it. I met another Punta driver in Ireland who told me that "Punta" is Gaelic for "cheap ass little car." That was pretty close. I felt that if I got a flat tire (sorry, a "puncture") I could just flip the Punta over on its side and go to work.

When we first picked up our car, the guy at the rental place handed me the keys and gave me a quick lesson in Irish driving. I remembered "Q" explaining the equipment to James Bond.

"That's the ignition. That's the wiper. The mirrors are on the side, you notice they collapse . . ."

He reached over to one of the side mirrors and clicked it back.

"If that happens, just do this."

He popped it back.

I would later learn that the pop-back mirrors are a very good idea if you are going to drive around in Ireland. I popped a lot of mirrors driving in Ireland. Sometimes going by stone walls, sometimes going by cows and sheep.

"You drive on the left side of the road, so when you get to

a roundabout remember that the cars to your right have the right of way. Good luck."

And with that, we were off.

I have never been much of a driver. I didn't have a license until I was twenty-three, and I am not skilled in the motor arts. Once I drove my friend Andy up to get some pizza. I had, at that time, a brand-new Toyota.

"Do you mind if I drive back?" he asked.

"No," I said. "Are you thinking about getting one of these cars?"

"No," he said. "I just don't want to sit in a car that you are driving."

That has happened to me many times since then. I have had people offer me money if they could just *"please, please, drive the goddamn car!"*

So I do not inspire confidence when I am behind the wheel. That was why I was surprised when Paulette wanted me to drive in Ireland. We drove off smiling. *What an adventure!*

After about ten minutes, ten minutes of nearly hitting a person, a building, a sign, or an animal (even bets in the West of Ireland) Paulette's face tightened a little. At twenty minutes she had the frozen stare of Mister Sardonicus.

Driving in Ireland is problematic. The main problem is all the two-lane roads look like lane-and-a-half roads. This makes driving in Ireland, especially in the rural west, a white-knuckle rock 'n' roll death trip. Most of the roads would not be able to handle John Goodman, Roger Ebert, and Marlon Brando walking along with arms linked like the Rockettes (this is, I grant you, an alarming image in its own right).

This is the Irish driving experience in short: You step out of a pub in the afternoon. You get into your car. You drive off through the beautiful, enchanting Irish countryside. All is well. Then you hear a voice next to you.

"Get on the left side!!!"

Then you die. At least you picked a good spot.

I found driving around in Ireland to be filled with near-death experiences. I thought they were stimulating after the plane ride. But, after just missing a little BMW outside Bally-vaughn, I was relieved of my driving duties.

"Let me drive!" Paulette finally screamed.

I could see that she was "concerned." "Sure," I said, and handed her the keys. I never felt better handing over anything. For the rest of the time, Paulette drove. We still had near-death experiences but since I wasn't driving I wasn't paying that much attention.

I had always thought that the outside scenes in movies about Ireland made the place look staggeringly beautiful, but I figured that the director carefully set up shots to emphasize that. The truth is, if you just walk around in the West of Ireland, everywhere you look there is a rare and beautiful view.

I am not a man who is very sensitive to that kind of thing: I walk with my head down, but it's just impossible not to notice how beautiful that place is. Mountains rising into the mist. Lakes and loughs seem to be placed for ultimate aesthetic effect. As they say, if God is an artist Ireland is some of his best work.

But things seem a little altered in the West of Ireland, a little unreal. Then you walk over a hill and a hundred sheep come walking up to you. Sheep seem to be wandering all over the place, and they never seem to be fenced in. I asked a young farmer about it.

"Are sheep allowed to just wander around?"

"Yes," he said, "them and the tourists."

We started out with a plan. For months we had talked about what we were going to do, how many trips we were making. (This part of the plan survived. We took one trip together, and I returned solo for a few weeks.) We planned this thing like they planned D-Day. We sharpened pencils and sat around the kitchen table drinking coffee, looking at maps, writing things down, drawing little lines, adding numbers, and calculating distances. By the time we were ready to go we had checked everything out big-time. We knew what the average temperature was, what the weather was likely to be. We knew where we were staying; we knew the precise exchange rate. We knew what things are supposed to cost in Ireland (so we didn't get cheated by any shifty Aran Island boys). We knew what we were doing. We were as prepared as Sir Edmund Hillary heading up Mount Everest.

We were dead set against any kind of preset "tour" or "itinerary." We had seen brochures and scoffed at their titles. "Finding the West," "Exploring Tipperary," "The Hidden Wonders of Innisfree." But we read a lot of travel guides and debated the details.

Once we got over there, however, everything changed. "Look at that," someone would say. Or, "Let's see what that is." And we would change our intricate plan. Then we started abandoning whole pieces of the plan and replacing them with spontaneous whims. We started to do this a lot. Then we started modifying our modifications.

Then we said something that is very easy to say in Ireland. We said to hell with the plan. After only two days, the plan was like the 1969 senior prom: a big hazy memory that you actually *try* to forget.

So we drove on, not quite senselessly, but much more randomly than we had anticipated back when we were looking at brochures and sharpening pencils. If you accept "make it up as you go" as a sort of "antiplan," that is the way to approach Ireland. Ireland itself was, after all, made up as they went.

Ireland is, however, a little country, so if you spend three weeks there, you could say that, generally speaking, you've seen the whole country. You wouldn't have spent much time anywhere, but you at least would have seen every place in the country. However, that is absolutely the worst way to see Ireland. The best way to do it involves, for many Americans, a little mindset work, but it's worth it.

The first step involves getting rid of almost any plan. Just imagine that you are getting into an inner tube and drifting around a big lake. You drift around anywhere the lake happens to take you. You don't rule anything out. You start each day not knowing where you're going to be sleeping that night. There is no goal, no plan. This is a dance, not a race.

So we knew we wanted to find out about my mom and dad. Except for that, we were in the lake drifting around and enjoying it, and that was the only plan. Our neatly plotted itinerary, drafted weeks before, staying in the bottom of my suitcase.

Early in our trip we went out to the Aran Islands. We had wanted to see them since our college days when we watched *Man of Aran*, Robert Flaherty's famous documentary. That movie left a lasting impression on Paulette and me. At the time, we were staying in a little house out in the country outside Athens, Georgia. We were attempting to survive on the seventy-five dollars a week I made as a security guard at Anaconda Wire & Cable Company.

That was the late hippie era, and when I worked for Anaconda, I had hair down to the middle of my back and was politically slightly left of Marx and Engels. They would have never hired a guy with my Julia Roberts–like hair, but I "disguised" my hair. Every afternoon before I left for work Paulette would methodically bobby-pin my flaxen locks. Then I would cover them with a deluxe Kmart wig. I looked ridiculous. Of course I could have just gotten a haircut, but that was unthinkable for me in those days. Cut my hair? No way, man! I'm not selling out to the military industrial complex, man! Nixon cuts his hair.

Instead I wore the ridiculous wig at work. I looked like an idiot but my political ideology was intact.

At any rate, I think we were feeling a little underprivileged at the time. We already had our first daughter, Aimee, and it wasn't Ritz-type living. Our car cost $250, and every time it made a funny noise, my heart skipped a beat because I knew that my net worth was usually in the mid two figures. If the car went, I would have to consider a career in slavery.

I remember listening to the Sinatra album *My Cole Porter* during this era and thinking, *Hmm. These songs really aren't about the life I'm living, are they?*

The house we were living in rented for sixty-five dollars a month. It wasn't a bargain. There was a two-foot hole in the floor in the living room. The heating was not state of the art. I remember sitting in the living room in winter and noticing that whenever I talked, steam came out of my mouth.

Anyway, despite our financial situation, it was a lot better than living in the Aran Islands. We watched *Man of Aran* on PBS's *Film Odyssey,* and we felt that we were living in comparative comfort. For an Aran Islander, I was a guy in a Cole Porter song fighting vainly the old ennui.

In the film, the Aran Islanders have it very tough. There isn't any dirt to grow potatoes, so every year they walk down to the shore and get the dirt. They put it in buckets and carry it back. Then they dump it into the cracks between the rocks and go back for more dirt.

This takes them a while. The film explained why they have to do this. Every year the ocean washes away all the soil, so the next year they have to put it back. This was farming where you had to go get the dirt first.

Then we see these men who go out in these little boats, called, I think, "curraghs," and catch sharks. These boats look very flimsy. They catch the sharks, which look like Jaws-size sharks, for the oil, not for the meat. A great number of the men get killed every year. But nobody complains. These are tough people.

After the film was over we cuddled together on our nine-dollar sofa. We had a two-foot hole in our living-room floor, but we felt plenty privileged. Life, I thought, is easy on a cool seventy-five a week.

Today, tourists go out to the Aran Islands. I think kids on

MTV Ireland go there on spring break. It's quite beautiful but still a bit scary. You can still feel the presence of all the people who have lived and died there. Some people say Flaherty exaggerated in his film. Not by much, I think. Old Aran Islanders talk about how tough it was back then. These young Aran Islanders don't know how easy they have it, I was told. I knew. I saw it on *Film Odyssey with Charles Champlin*.

I met an ex-Aran Islander in Georgia. He plays guitar at a faux-Irish pub in the Virginia Highlands area of Atlanta called "Limerick Junction." I asked him why he left his home.

"Are you kidding?" he asked, answering a question with a question in the classic Irish style.

The Aran that Paulette and I saw in that film has stayed in our minds. "Aran" has become for us shorthand for a truly bad time. When things were really awful—when the car broke down and we had no money or when it snowed and everybody got stomach flu at the same time—we could say to each other, "This is getting like Aran," and look at each other. Or one of us might say that a bad party was "like Aran" and be sure that one person understood. Now we were going to see the real Aran. I was almost sad that our little Aran was coming to an end. What if Aran was nice?

We headed out to the Aran Islands on a cloudy, windy day. It wasn't the best weather but if you wait for a sunny day in Ireland you may have a few birthdays before you get one.

I didn't get along well with water. I blame my dad for this. His theory of swimming education was this: Throw the kid in and see what happens. My older brother thrived with this plan, so my dad was pretty convinced of its efficacy by the time I showed up.

I remember my dad walking with me into the ocean. I was about five, but that day is permanently burned into the template of my mind. He kept walking until the water was up to my neck. The he picked me up and kept walking. When the water was up to his neck, he stopped.

"You're not going to throw me in, are you, Dad?" I asked nervously.

"Oh, no," he said, "I'm not going to do that."

Then, of course, he threw me in.

Thus I was B. F. Skinnered into my lifelong fear of water. I can swim, but I dream of drowning and I can't float on my back because I can never "trust" the water.

So the trip out to the Aran Islands was not a lot of laughs for me. Paulette wanted to do it, so we went.

"Just like in the movies," she said.

The Aran Islands are three little islands at the mouth of Galway Bay. They run a sort of ferry out to them (it's a couple of miles). The ferry is always pretty full.

We got in the ferry-type boat and headed out. Everyone seemed to be smiling. I heard people around me speaking English and French and Spanish and German. When we got about a hundred yards from the shore a little voice in my brain started telling me that I was about to die. I remembered that John Synge's play *Raiders to the Sea* is set in the Aran Islands. In the play there is an old woman. Many of her sons have drowned in the past. At the beginning of the play she has one son left. He drowns right before the curtain.

I looked over at Paulette. She was smiling like a kid at the circus. I watched nervously as we approached an island. I was horrified when we kept going to a more distant island. Why couldn't we take the first one, for God's sake? One Aran Island is as good as another, isn't it? Give a hydrophobic guy a break!

I was very happy to get off that boat, and we stumbled out to inspect the island. I looked around. I had never heard of an island sinking, so I felt a little better.

We had landed on Inishmore, the largest of the islands. I was surprised to see that there were people who lived there. Somehow I had thought that everybody would have moved (or drowned), but there were a lot of people there. Most of them are (still) involved in fishing, although, truth be told, tourism is the main source of income there.

A lot of the boats that aren't carrying tourists are carrying peat. The boats are called "hookers." I heard the word used by a guide, and I was, for a moment, extremely confused. I spent most of my time on the island confused. In the Aran Islands Gaelic is the everyday language. I kept trying to over-hear conversations because Irish people have the same bouncy cadence to their voices no matter what language is spoken. I'd have to get pretty close to tell it wasn't English.

The island is very beautiful. It doesn't look typically "Irish" there. It also doesn't look anything like *Man of Aran*. I started to wonder if Flaherty had faked the whole thing. Maybe *Man of Aran* was shot on the same soundstage as the faked moon landing?

On the Aran Islands the "gray rocks" have taken over, and green is a rare sight. There are a lot of ruins of ancient forts, a few churches, and a medieval monastery. I was surprised to see cows and pigs. I was startled to see that there was a small landing strip. Soon, I thought, I will come across a theme park.

Through body language I was able to convey to Paulette the idea that I didn't want to stay long. I also wanted to see if I could avoid boats for the rest of the trip (and, with luck, the rest of my life).

After getting back on land, I resisted the temptation to bend over and kiss it. We got in the Punta and drove. Our destination was a famous Irish landmark, the Cliffs of Moher.

The ride there was pretty spectacular. A lot of Ireland's coastline is cliffs and promontories, and this particular little trip is a cruise right on the edge of a rocky coastline with a drop of several hundred feet. We stopped a few times and got out of the car and looked out at some seriously mysterious stuff.

There are a lot of little islands out there. Nobody lives on them—too rugged for even an Aran Islander. The islands are called "the Blasket." They look like the peaks of submerged mountains right after the Noah incident.

Sidetracked at the Burren

On our way to the Cliffs of Moher, we got sidetracked. "Sidetracked" is a strange word, but it conveys almost exactly what most of our driving-around time was like. We might as well have driven sideways.

Asking for directions in Ireland is a remarkable activity. When we stopped to ask somebody how to get to someplace, the guy would usually try to anticipate *why* we were going there. If we asked to go to the bathroom a rappin' Irish guy might say:

"Is it urinating you're anticipating?"

We stopped and asked an old man with a red cloth jacket directions to the Cliffs of Moher. He may have been looking after his sheep or cows, but there was only one sheep in sight. The sheep had a dab of blue paint in his wool. (You see that a lot in the West of Ireland. While I was in Ireland I asked three people why they color the sheep. I received three completely different, complicated answers. Suffice it to say, the Irish color the sheep for "reasons of their own.")

The man was very friendly. He started to tell us how to get to the Cliffs of Moher. He kept asking questions that began, "Are you familiar with . . ." We would shake our heads with a vacant stare. He kept trying.

He kept mentioning a place called "the Burren." I asked him if the Burren was good to see. I remembered it being mentioned in one of the guidebooks.

"Oh, yes," he said.

So we went to the Burren. It wasn't far.

It turned out to be a very good sidetrack. The Burren is one of the oddest places I have ever seen. It's a large (116 square miles) area of rolling limestone hills that doesn't look like anyplace in Ireland. It really doesn't even look like earth. Except for a tree here and there it is absolutely nothing but flat rock as far as the eye can see.

"Burren" means "rocky land" in Gaelic. The place may have been formed out of the skeletons of animals that lived here millions of years ago. A walk across the Burren is a very strange experience. If you ever wanted to "get away from it all," this would be the place. You see an occasional little plant growing out of the limestone; otherwise nothing. By "nothing," I mean "Nothing." Less than Samuel Beckett's emptiest room.

There are caves all over, but the only one we inspected was the one with the handrails installed for touring cavern fans. They've built an environment-blended building around it, so today it looks like an ancient subway entrance. I didn't go far. One cave is as good as another.

They offer tours of the cave, the Ailween Cave, although business seemed slow on that particular day. I was not shocked. You rarely hear, "I went to Ireland for the caves."

There are (as in a whole lot of places in Ireland) a lot of megalithic tombs and Celtic crosses around the Burren and there is an actual monastery, a twelfth-century one called Corcomroe. As you walk around you see the remains of little villages that were deserted during the potato famine. If you spend enough time in the Burren you can forget what century it is. We walked around for an hour or so, and I started to feel I was in an early scene of *Planet of the Apes: The Irish Part.*

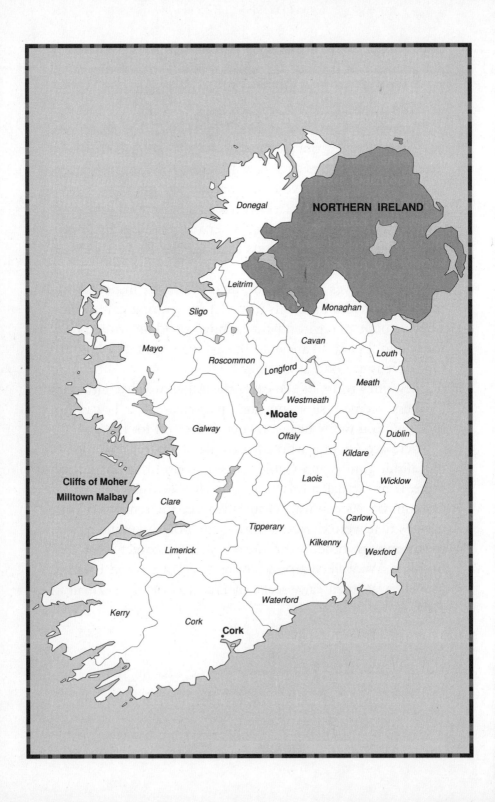

SIX

～ *Brave New World* ～

Ireland is this:

- Connacht—Galway, Leitrim, Mayo, Roscommon, Sligo
- Leinster—Carlow, Dublin, Kildare, Kilkenny, Laois, Longford, Louth, Meath, Offaly, Westmeath, Wexford, Wicklow
- Munster—Clare, Cork, Kerry, Limerick, Tipperary, Waterford
- Ulster—Antrim, Armagh, Cavan, Donegal, Down, Fermanagh, Londonderry, Monaghan, Tyrone

Antrim, Armagh, Down, Fermanagh, Londonderry, and Tyrone are technically part of England, but they're attached to the island, so I include them. "Northern Ireland" is a really confusing concept. It's not really "Northern Ireland"; it's part of Northern Ireland. At any rate, it's a little country. I am not Daniel Boone by any means (I get lost walking in my neighborhood) and I had all of the counties snugly in my cranium after just a few days.

Out in the West of Ireland things look pretty much the way it looks in that picture that forms in your mind when someone says "Ireland." There also seems to be a quality that is floating in the general atmosphere: "Irishness."

"Irishness" is discussed as if it were an actual palpable thing. You hear people in little pubs in Galway saying things like, "We're losing our Irishness," or, "He lost his Irishness." "Irishness," when lost, is always an occasion for sorrow. People express fear of losing their Irishness. If you're lucky enough to have it, you want to hang on to it.

Having observed people talking about Irishness, I draw certain conclusions:

- Irishness, when put into words, sounds poetic. It often involves sheep, heather, rainbows, stone walls, and thatch-roofed cottages.
- Irishness can be faked. Americans can't tell fake Irishness from real Irishness, but all Irish people can. The fake Irishness is so obvious to them they often laugh derisively when they see it.
- "Irishness" is an endangered species.

The southwest of Ireland is a place you could stay forever. It was there that I first felt that little hand on the shoulder telling me that even though you've never been here, this is the place for you. Paulette, who is 1 percent Irish, felt the same thing. There are many startling things there.

On a cliff edge in a place called Liscannor there is a pretty spectacular tower. It's what is left of a castle built in the fifteenth century. It was originally built as a place to spot the enemy, who were, at that time, the Spanish. The Spanish never showed up, but the amazing tower is still there. The rest of the castle is, as the kids say, history.

The view from the tower is beautiful. It looks out over the Atlantic Ocean. This is appropriate because, I was told, the man who invented the submarine was from the little village of Liscannor. There is a plaque that commemorates the man. He thought that his invention would help the United States in their fight against . . . guess who? (England. Shocked?)

Not far from there we saw a monastery at Dysert O'Dea. There is a wall that is decorated at the top with little carved faces. They've let this one deteriorate. This isn't surprising when you consider just how many ancient ruins there are in Ireland.

The monastery is almost thirteen hundred years old, but the Ozymandias-like faces are still up there: an arc of ancient faces staring at you. Almost all of them are frowning. One face looks as if he's about to laugh. Whenever there are ten Irish faces together there is always one wise ass.

Paulette had to make me leave. There was something in the faces that riveted me. Did the sculptor make that guy smile? Or was it just erosion? I like to think that erosion produced the smile, like God correcting the artist's work.

Near the Cliffs of Moher there is a little place called Lisdoonvarna. This is the place, I think, that evoked the Janeane Garofalo movie, *The Matchmaker*. In Lisdoonvarna, the ancient elaborate mate-finding ritual is still "followed" (at least it is an excuse for a festival). The movie left a lot to be desired, but there is a beautiful tower that looks just like the sort of tower they use in Errol Flynn movies. Like so many other Irish towers, it looks out over the ocean. I don't know what invader they had in mind. It should have been used to prevent the producers of *The Matchmaker* from ever getting a foothold.

The Cliffs of Moher

The ride to the Cliffs of Moher is really beautiful. If I had had a convertible I would have put the top down. (We would have gotten wet, but we were beginning to accept "wet" as the usual Irish condition. You get wet, you sit in front of a turf fire, you get dry, you go outside, you get wet. Rinse. Repeat.)

We enjoyed that beautiful ride so much that we forgot, for a second, that we were driving along on a two-lane road that was twelve feet wide. We cruised around Liscannor Bay and, as we went along, we saw more and more signs for the Cliffs of Moher.

The Cliffs of Moher are a great natural phenomenon and, like all great American natural phenomena, it has a parking lot. We parked at a visitors' center and got out of the Punta, glad to get the chance to straighten our legs. I looked back at the Punta. It looked like the kind of car twelve clowns get out of.

The cliffs are quite amazing. They go seven hundred feet straight out of the ocean, and, at every level, they are covered with tourists. When we got there, there were at least three hundred people there. There are railings so tourists don't fall into the Atlantic Ocean. I asked a guy at the snack shop and he told me that, as far as he knows, only one tourist had ever taken the big plunge, and he believed it was intentional, although he wasn't sure.

Paulette doesn't like heights, but she accompanied me to the highest points of the Cliffs of Moher. There is a very impressive tower up there, built by MP Sir Cornelius O'Brian in the nineteenth century. They let you go up into the tower and the view from up there is quite spectacular. Paulette let me know, in a subtle way, when it was time to leave the tower and its spectacular view. She let me know by hitting me in the ribs in a Jake LaMotta manner.

When we got to the bottom we noticed several parked vans selling CDs and T-shirts. Paulette went off to the bathroom. When she was gone I struck up a conversation with a guy in a CD van. He was about six-six with tight curly black hair. His T-shirt said "Manhattan, The Greatest City in the World."

I asked him all about the cliffs and his life. He was from Bunraty. He played rhythm guitar in a band. They played in bars. I asked him a lot of questions. He answered them politely. Then he asked me a question.

"Why are you asking me all these questions?"

"I'm writing a book," I said. "I just need the facts, sir." I tried to sound like Jack Webb in *Dragnet* as a friendly, bantering thing. He didn't get it.

"Do you know *Dragnet* here?"

"Sure." A pause. "Oh, you were doing a Jack Webb thing. That's funny."

I saw Paulette returning from the bathroom. The wind was lifting her hair. It was now just starting to rain.

"I gotta get out of here," I said. I shook his hand.

"There aren't any facts in Ireland," he said. He waved goodbye.

But there are some facts. William Faulkner said that the past wasn't really past. There is no place on earth where Faulkner's statement is truer than in Ireland. But first, let's just look at the physical place.

Ireland is an island, "John Bull's other island." It's set out there apart from the rest of Europe next to that other island, England. But Ireland is its own little, intensely green place.

The oldest definition we have for the word "Eriu," the source of the word "Ireland," is often translated as something like "the most beautiful woman in the world," which is pretty appropriate because Ireland is really good looking. If we personify countries, and the United States is Uncle Sam, and Russia is either a bear or a rotund "Mother Russia," Ireland is "the most beautiful woman in the world."

If Ireland were a woman, she would be a very good one to date. She is a knockout. The most beautiful woman in the world. She walks down the street and breaks hearts.

Ireland is known by many names, but none of them, except "Eriu," is a woman's name, although sometimes, in songs, they refer to Ireland as "she." The country is sometimes called "The Emerald Isle," "The Old Country," "The Old Sod," or "Erin." My dad, who referred to England only as "jolly old England," called Ireland all of those names and a few other less pleasant ones. But my dad never referred to it as a warm, inviting place. He often referred to it like a place he escaped from, an old woman whose clutches he evaded.

Whatever you call it, magical land or penal colony, when

you approach the island in an airplane, or look at it from a
boat far offshore, it seems like an enclosed, very separate en-
tity, a different world, a theme park made by God. "Mist
Land." "Planet Green." "The Land of Saints and Scholars."
"Island of the Religious Drinkers." Too bad "Greenland" is
taken.

Ireland's coastline is 2,000 miles, pretty remarkable when
you consider how little the country is. From the tip of Ulster
to the shore of Kerry, it's only about 350 miles. From north-
west to southwest, it's about 200 miles. A little place, really.
A little bigger than New Jersey, smaller than Georgia.

Planet Green is a theme park with a lot of water. Eight
hundred lakes. The River Shannon, its main river, is really a
huge interlocking network of rivers and lakes. So, if you add
in the fact that it rains almost every day, you can safely say
that if you are in Ireland, you are close to water no matter
where you are. In fact, if you are in Ireland, you are probably wet. When people speak of the "Shannon dampness,"
they are describing the place very well, and they are very close
to the heart of Ireland. The average yearly rainfall in Ireland
is over thirty inches a year, and the idea of dampness comes
up in countless Irish sayings.

Irish people are wet a lot, although they, as a rule, don't
do much swimming. Ireland, for all that water, isn't big on
water sports. Oddly, Irish people aren't that fond of fish. I
met an Irish surfer, two words that don't seem to belong together. I asked him how he did that, and he said, "Drunk."

There is not a spot in Ireland more than a hundred miles
to the sea, and you would have to look very hard to find a
place in Ireland ten miles from a river or a lake or a pond or
a stream. Unless you stay inside all the time, it's hard to stay
completely dry in Ireland. I took a lot of pictures when I was
in Ireland, a lot of pictures of wet people.

It almost never snows there. If it does, it's gone in an hour
or two. No skiing. But lots and lots of mist. Wake up early in

Ireland; look out the window at the green mist. It does seem like another planet.

Because of all that water, Ireland looks really, really, well, green. But there are many shades of green in Ireland. How many shades? The standard answer is "forty." I was told "seventy-one" by a man in glasses in a pub in Longford. I believe him. The preciseness of "seventy-one" convinced me.

Whatever the number, the sheer *greenness* is overwhelming, and if you stare at green for a long time it begins to affect your vision.

In Ireland, there are always gray skies and gray rocks that seem to set off the green, so the landscape almost glows when you look at a long horizon. I have lived for a long time in the rural South of America, and I have seen lots of pastures and farms. But Ireland doesn't look like the American South. I told a man in Ireland that Ireland looks a lot like Scotland and he looked at me as if I was insane or just really, really stupid. Ireland or Scotland? Apples and oranges. If you can't tell them apart you are a sad case.

The Old Sod has a very distinctive look. The green is broken up on the ground by—always—some rocks, some gray rocks. There are gray stones everywhere. And where there aren't gray stones, there are gray ruins, of ancient buildings. And on the sides of the ancient crumbling gray walls there are green ivy vines. And where there aren't rock or ruins there are little winding gray roads. And there always seems to be the ocean, or a stream, or a lake, or a pond, somewhere in the background to add some hazy, vaguely mysterious blue.

I am not a poet, but when I looked at Ireland I started to have what I called "poetic thoughts." (I kept these, largely, to myself.)

Anyway, trust me. Ireland doesn't look like anyplace else.

Ireland has what geography people call a temperate climate. Parts of the southwest actually have some tropical flora stuff that wouldn't look out of place in Florida.

The average temperature, for the whole year, in Ireland is

fifty degrees Fahrenheit, but, as I was told, "Every day in Ireland is all four seasons." It will be freezing in the morning, but you will sweat before the day is through. After a few days in Ireland I went with the "layers" strategy: a T-shirt, a regular shirt, a thin sweater, a thick sweater, a coat. You get the idea. It worked pretty well. You are always putting things on and taking them off in Ireland. You sweat and shiver three hours apart.

"Ireland is a natural simulacrum of a detox center." I was told this by a man in a bar near Athlone. He had a huge, bulbous nose, and it looked as if he knew what he was talking about.

Ireland was an island before Britain became an island. Because of this, there are certain plants in Ireland that do not appear in Britain. This also accounts for certain differences in the animals found on the two islands. And, Yes! There are no snakes in Ireland! I wasn't able to establish whether there had ever been any there. I was told, of course, that the island was crawling with snakes until Saint Patrick got rid of them. Scientists believe that there never were any there to start with, but I wouldn't necessarily buy that.

Irish people have an odd relationship with the weather. Most Americans think that a rainy day is bad, but the Irish people I talked to actually seemed to like the rain. The best day to Irish people is a day where the rain is misting, a "grand soft day." You see happy faces when it's raining in Ireland, something you would never see in, say, Philadelphia. You don't know what dark thoughts the Irish may be thinking, but the Irish people do smile a lot.

Almost all of the houses in the Irish countryside seem to be white. This also serves to set off the amazing glowing greenness that surrounds everything. If you are a fat slob in Ireland, dark green is a good fashion choice (avoid white or gray at all costs).

In fiction and movies, Ireland seems to be a hilly place. It is, but not many of the hills get very big. I was surprised to find out that only three of Ireland's mountains exceed three thousand feet. They aren't big hills, but there are a lot of them; you are never far from a hill or a mound or a small mountain, and there always seems to be one looming in the background. It's hard to take a picture of the Irish countryside that doesn't have some little mountain or hill behind whatever you're taking a picture of.

So it's gray and white and green. Everything else is just several different shades of green with dots of gray and white. After a whole day of rambling around the Irish countryside, you get very used to long uninterrupted green. When you close your eyes, it's still green. Then you drink some Guinness. Walk outside. Close your eyes. Open them. The green doesn't go away.

Whatever else it is, Ireland is great to look at, one of the great places in the world to go for a long bike ride. Throughout history, God's deal with the Irish seems to have been, "You get a really pretty country, but that's it. You get no optional equipment."

The Irish people have always worked extremely hard for very little. The land is tough farming because it's so damn rocky and hilly. Most of the land requires a whole lot of preparation before you could even think about farming.

Irish people consider a field without any rocks to be a wonderful thing. A man can be proud of his field because it took him countless hours to get all those rocks out of it. There is no farmland in Ireland like the great wide-open plains of the Midwest in America. Farming Ireland has always been absolutely brutal work.

Unlike Wales and Britain and Scotland, Ireland has almost no coal or iron ore. The Industrial Revolution in Ireland was a very quiet affair. The country does have more peat (sod that is burned for heat and not for electricity), than anyplace else in Europe. You can always see huge fields of peat being cut in vast thin rows. The smell of burning peat instantly evokes home for anybody who grew up in Ireland. If there is an "Irish smell," it's peat burning.

At one time Ireland had as much as 311,000 hectares of bogland, land you could cut up for fuel. Today these bog-lands are disappearing fast. In twenty years, people told me, the bogs and the peat will be gone.

Peat fires are a big part of the "romantic" picture of Ire-land's past that movies have helped to produce, but I'm sure that Irish people would rather have had the unromantic coal, or, better yet, oil.

But if the peat will be gone soon, no one in Ireland seems overly concerned. If you mention "the peat crisis," you are met with no alarm. You are told that Ireland has continually run out of things throughout history. The things it didn't run out of, it didn't have. So don't sweat it.

A woman in Cashel told me, "We've never had enough of anything, ever. We don't even know what it's like to have enough of anything. So big deal with no peat."

There never seems to be a "Plan B" in Ireland. The dom-inant attitude of the Irish people is definitely more grasshop-per than ant.

The West of Ireland is still basically a land of country peo-ple. The houses tend to be pretty far apart because most of the people used to, or still do, have farms of one sort or an-other. The archetypal west Irish person's neighbors live maybe a half-mile away.

I think some Irish people tend to like it that way. That may have something to do with the "Cold Irish" thing. My uncle John told me, when I was a kid, "If an Irishman is all warm and huggy, he's drunk."

Maybe. Other people told me that the houses are far apart so that the women won't talk to each other all day. Both of these theories need work.

Ireland's geography is not complex. There are four provinces in Ireland: Leinster in the east, Munster in the southwest, Connaught in the west, and Ulster (home of the "troubles") in the north. "The north" as the home of the "troubles" isn't quite accurate. People are quick to tell you that the northernmost point in Ireland is actually part of the republic. Long ago, in the Middle Ages, they wrote about a fifth province in the middle, Meath or Midland, but that distinction is long gone. "There are four provinces in Ireland" is a truism.

In ancient times, the northern half of Ireland was known as Leth Cuinn ("Conn's side": Conn was a mythological hero). The southern half of Ireland was known as Leth Moga (named after another mythical personage, Mug Nuadat).

("Mug Nuadat," by the way, sounds like a character in a James Cagney gangster movie. While I was writing this book, I stopped and looked through cast lists of old movies to see if some Irish-American screenwriter decided to be a wise guy, but I never found a "Mug Nuadat" in any of those Dead End Kids/Gangster movies.)

Speaking of "Mug Nuadat," the Irish approach to names is a lot different than the American. My name, "Francis Xavier Gannon," passes for an "Irish name." But a *really* Irish name is something like "Aoife Cullinane." And Irish people pronounce a lot of names much differently than you might think. "Kathleen" is always "Katt-lean," for instance. You come across unpronounceable first names like "Ciaran" ("Key-er-un"), "Aine" ("own-ya"), and "Siobahn ("shy-von") on a regular basis. When confronted with an unpronounceable Gaelic name, I found a simple solution. Speak fast and slur.

They're used to a language called Celtic (KELL-TIC). I had heard it was dead but I was assured by several people in Ireland that it is as alive as Britney Spears. It's spoken in small areas all over the world, but in Ireland it's still used in Donegal, Mayo, and Galway.

Gaelic is a language that is actually growing in usage. The Irish government subsidizes it, and it's in many school curricula in Ireland. If you want to get a long, difficult-to-follow argument, ask someone in Ireland why "Gaelic" is called "Irish" in many parts of Ireland, and "Gaelic" in some others. Like the people everywhere I've been, these people are very touchy on the subject of language.

I was never a very good speller. In the statewide spelling bee, an event in which my brother qualified for the finals, I went out on the word "whip," which I spelled "wip." For me, spell-check is a great invention. In Ireland, however, good spellers have my unreserved awe.

Consider the word "winter," a simple little word used in everyday speech. In Gaelic "winter" is spelled "*geimhreadh*." It is pronounced something like "Ja-year-ee." The winner of a Gaelic spelling competition is a child who may, in time, rule the world.

Giant Irish Stones

The past in Ireland isn't remote because every few minutes you seem to come across something really old. In America *really* old is the Liberty Bell. But in Ireland really old is really old. There are literally thousands of megalithic monuments in Ireland, and there are many towers and churches that are over a thousand years old. I live near Atlanta. In Atlanta they have plans to tear things down by the time they are finished building. But in Ireland you are continually drawn back into the past every time you turn a corner.

Ireland is an archaeologist's dream. When we first started rambling around and we came to some ancient giant stones that looked like Stonehenge, we stopped and had a look. After a while we were passing them by. If you drive for twenty minutes the odds are you are going to encounter some megalithic tomb.

There are so many of these partly because much of Ireland has been left pretty much alone. I am relatively sure that all megalithic work has vanished from, say, New Jersey. Where I grew up Stonehenge would have been imploded a long time ago.

People really aren't sure why these giant things were built in the first place. It seems likely that there was some religious meaning behind the massive things. The sheer size of the things is amazing. I was told that some of the stones weigh a hundred tons.

Paulette and I used one for something that they are often used for today: human sacrifice. Just kidding. We had our picture taken in front of it. The massive thing is called Crevy-keel. It's in Sligo. Right now I bet somebody from America is standing in front of it smiling.

At night these massive things take on a different aspect, as if some gigantic thing is about to appear and sit down next to his giant rock table. A lot of archaeologists have pointed out that these massive stone groups are often placed in a way that links them to astronomical movement. The ancient people weren't mysteriously "advanced" like in those shows narrated by Leonard Nimoy. The ancient Irish just spent a lot of time looking at the sky, looking at "the big picture."

Ireland itself seems to lead you to look at things from a different, more distant perspective. In Ireland my little human life suddenly seemed very, very brief.

Taking the long approach (very long) yields another perspective on Ireland. Looking at things from God's perspective, Ireland is sort of a saucer without a teacup. The Irish, like their friendly neighbors, have made the "tea" into a constant, and they are constantly using it as a metaphor.

As God sits down to his afternoon repast, He looks over at Ireland and sees the cup and permanently raises it to His lips. He takes a sip. If you are a deist, he leaves the cup out in the Cosmos somewhere and takes a nap. Maybe this is something else, but the middle of Ireland is a sort of round, flat circle in the middle, surrounded by a little ridge of mountains.

It hasn't always been God's teacup and saucer. A million and a half years ago, Ireland was linked to Europe and covered with ice. Before that it was actually probably attached to North America. But, as the eons sped by, it got a little warmer, and Ireland, now an island, floated off to begin the saucer portion of its life and to become its own little place, Planet Green.

Around ten thousand years ago the first people arrived, strolling over the few tiny land bridges that connected Ireland to what is now Europe. (If it had stayed attached to Europe, things might be very different. Today, Irish people might like Jerry Lewis movies, like to think of names for cheese, drink a lot of red wine, and make existential comments. "Irish Cooking" might no longer be the answer in the "thinnest book" joke. There might have been no "pomme de terre" famine.)

Extremely early Irish history is pretty misty. There are, however, a few things left that serve as clues. There are, for instance, lots of remains of the ancient giant deer they call the Irish elk. It seems safe to say that ancient Ireland was covered with these deer. The oldest traces of Irish human life are in Ulster, in the valley of the river Boyne. The original inhabitants of Ireland were, it is believed, hunter-gatherers, who lived near the ocean and used some very primitive tools, and, of course, built giant stone tombs.

Many Irish megalithic tombs are covered with what seem to be symbols. There are whorls and spirals and all sorts of elaborate embellishments. No one knows the exact meaning of these things, but there are lots of speculative explanations. The people must have had some belief system, and these structures must have meant something to them, but all of that is lost.

These giant tombs originally contained multiple dead people, and these are actually the oldest man-made constructions in the world. They are older than the pyramids, and about one thousand years older than Stonehenge. Whatever else is true about them, the ancient Irish honored their dead.

Early Irish history sounds like a great number of invasions,

but most historians think that it was much more peaceful
than the word "invasion" usually connotes. Different groups
came and stayed, but there wasn't massive carnage. If there
can be peaceful invasions, that's what Ireland experienced.

Each group of new people brought innovations and
changes, and the culture changed in very small increments.
Most of the invaders spoke variations of the same language,
so early in Ireland's history you don't find anything like 1066
in England, where a whole new culture takes over.

The Bronze Age in Ireland was very long, almost fifteen
centuries, and there are a lot of amazing ancient Irish bronze
weapons and ornaments. By 100 B.C. Ireland was dominated
by a race called the "Fir Bolg." The "Fir Bolg" were replaced
by the people that are still there, "the Celts." (When you are
in Ireland do not pronounce the word *Selts*. I did and was
told by an Aran Islander that "The *Selts* are a basketball team;
the *Kelts* are a people.")

By looking at Irish myths of this era scholars have pieced
together a general picture. In Irish mythology, kings are always "marrying" divine entities, usually described as "goddesses." The goddesses guide the kings. By 150 B.C. the Celts
were the dominant group, but it was far from a unified country. The Celts are described in history books as fair-skinned,
with red hair. Their language was, like English, Germanic.
Eventually several distinct dialects evolved. The variety called
by linguists "Q-Celts" is the one that prevailed. The English
language is ancient in Ireland. Despite what some people say,
English as a language is not something that was "imposed"
on the people by outsiders.

The Celts were, like most ancient people, polytheistic.
They had over four hundred gods. Some of them have well-
known Greek equivalents. The Irish god Esus is something
close to Hermes, the messenger god, and Taranis ("thun-
der") was the head god, an Irish version of Zeus. There was
a god for almost every natural phenomenon, and the land itself was deified, as were the larger rivers. It was pantheistic,

but there were a few gods that seem to have little to do with nature.

The Celts were not a tightly unified group. There were little tribes and bands that were self-contained and sometimes fought with each other. A band was called a *tuath*. Frequently, a *tuath* had its own god. The Celts that settled in central Europe were a powerful military force with a reputation for absolute ruthless savagery in battle. The Irish version of the Celts highly valued military force, but they seem to have been a bit mellower than their continental variety.

They had pretty much a common culture. They seem to have liked exaggerated figures of speech, and had an odd tendency to categorize things in terms of threes. (This habit of mind recalls the old myth about Saint Patrick using the three-petaled shamrock to teach about the Trinity: three Beings in one God.)

The Irish mythological version of the old days goes something like this: The three sons of King Mileadth, aka "the Milesians" invaded Ireland about the time of Alexander the Great and defeated the Tuatha De Danann, who had earlier defeated the Fir Bolg. Around 100 B.C. the Gaels arrived, and, from then on, all of the Gaelic kings tried to trace their lineage back to the "Milesians." The arrival of the Gaels, again, wasn't an invasion. They just blended in with the Celts. After a while the Gaels were actually called Celts.

The structure of the civilization that the ancient Irish developed sounds, to many people (and me), strangely appealing. Their system, whatever else it is, is the sort of thing that (except for slavery and an occasional human sacrifice here and there) sounds "good on paper." Once in a while an "outsider" politician in America will cite that ancient Irish system as a good model. I think that Norman Mailer alluded to the system a few times during his bizarre run for mayor of New York in the sixties. Jimmy Breslin, his running mate and a certified mick, may have been an influence.

The societal and legal order went something like this:

There were several social classes: Among them were the Brehons, who were the judges and lawmakers. The Brehons were forbidden to have any economic interests in the system. They didn't really "own" anything, but they had a high social position, and their needs were taken care of by society. They were truly "disinterested." There was no need for campaign finance reform.

Under the Brehon Law, a man was judged as a member of a tribe and a family. Justice was meted out to various groups without much consideration of a person as an individual. The only people who were treated that way under the law were the "men of Art and Learning." This lack of recognition of the individual and his rights was definitely a shortcoming of the system.

The symbols of wealth were cattle and land. Land could not be transferred, however. The same family held the same lands whatever the members of that family might do. Land was unlosable; cattle, however, could be sold or lost. Slavery was widely practiced, as it was almost everywhere else in the world at that time. There was capital punishment. There was also banishment, which was, under the conditions, almost as bad as a death sentence. One person would have had a brutally hard time surviving without the society even though most of the population lived quite apart from each other.

There were a lot of "wars," but these wars were really more like ancient "lawsuits." Many of them seem to have been settled by judges and agreements. Bloodshed was rare.

If you read contemporary accounts of the era, the amazingly lofty language that is used really makes an impression. Mundane things are given an almost cosmic dimension. The accounts sound like King Arthur and his court or *The Lord of the Rings,* but the reality was probably much different. It you look at the way life was really lived (the typical life lived in a little cavelike dwelling), you are astounded at the Irish tendency to make everything sound much more "profound" than it really is. Centuries later, when James Joyce turned a working day in Dublin into an epic Homeric journey, he was, in a way, doing something typically "Irish." An Irishman from this era would be very comfortable with Joyce's "inflation" of everyday events.

There were several clearly defined classes. The priests were, of course, the Druids. The Fili were poets, storytellers, and historians. Most of the other people belonged to either the free noble class or the unfree peasants, who were slaves, laborers, and workingmen.

The law was called "*gavelkind.*" Under this system, even though families stayed on the same piece of land forever, land could not be privately "owned." Like the Native Americans, the ancient Irish saw land as something that God "rents" to us. Families had rights to the land they worked, but this was not ownership.

The noble class, operating under the direction of the Brehons, elected the "king." And that's pretty much the skeleton of the system.

Except for a few problems, this was a remarkably facile system, and it worked very well for a long time. One aspect of this society that is fascinating (and almost unique among ancient people) is the high position that women occupied in the culture. They also placed a great value on learning, and eloquence was considered a great gift from the gods. (The twentieth century is, in literature, pretty much Ireland's century, but words have always been very close to the Irish heart. My uncle John told me that there was a writer in every pub in Ireland, and I think he was pretty close.)

The warrior class was required to observe something similar to the Arthurian code of courtly behavior. One part of the oath requires a Celtic warrior to never back down if he is confronted by fewer than ten foes. Even in their codes they like to inflate things.

Around A.D. 200, a man named Conn Ced-cathach established the kingdom of Munster in the south of Ireland. His descendant, Niall, is often regarded as the first king (Ard Ri) of Ireland, but he wasn't a king in the usual sense. His word wasn't law throughout Ireland. But his descendants were the dominant force in Ireland until Brian Boru at the end of the tenth century.

The period usually called the Dark Ages, the time from the fall of Rome to the crowning of Charlemagne, is, for many, Ireland's Golden Age. Ireland was arguably the intellectual center of the world in the seventh and eighth centuries.

It is a long time since the days of *gavelkind*, but today's Ireland also seems, in a way, much more civilized than America. If George Bush the first went to the West of Ireland, he would see a "kinder and gentler" place.

Civilization in Northern Ireland is, of course, always on the verge of complete collapse. In the rest of Ireland (which is the only real "Ireland"), things are very peaceful. The crime rate is very low, much lower than in America. The Irish people I met in Atlanta all shared one common reaction to America: It's amazingly violent in the land of the free!

In the rural parts of Ireland crime seems almost absent, but I became aware of one social problem. There is a whole disenfranchised group of people in Ireland that exist almost completely outside the law. One of the puzzling problems of western Ireland is, it seems, "the tinkers." When first introduced to the term, Paulette and I, Yanks that we are, did not know what a tinker was. We both thought a "tinker" was a guy who fixed small things. That is the origin of the term "tinker," but in Ireland it now means something much darker.

The Tinkers

Bridie Levins, one of our many landladies, told us that she usually keeps her front door open.

"Unless, of course," she told me with some gravity, "the tinkers are coming."

I nodded as if I understood.

"And of course, I have to take the flowers in," she said without any further explanation, as if everyone in his right mind would know why you had to bring in the flowers when the tinkers were about.

All through our stay in the west, the tinkers were alluded to. People would say things like, "Be sure you're out of there by four. I hear there are some tinkers coming in around four." And, "Don't park your car there, a bunch of tinkers are going to be passing by." And, "You don't want to be going to that place. That's a tinker hangout."

But no one told me what the hell the tinkers were, and why I should be so wary of them. Were they the Irish equivalent of the Hells Angels? The Celtic Crips? One afternoon, I had my chance to find out.

It was a cold, overcast day in Moat, a little village near the middle of Ireland. I was in a pub when I got the word. Some tinkers were about to arrive. I noticed the streets seemed emptier than usual. It was like high noon. Soon, I thought, these tinkers will come riding in. Although I still did not know what the tinkers were, I did not feel very Gary Cooperish.

The town clock tolled twelve times.

Tinker time.

There were two large cops (whom Irish people refer to as "the guard") standing at a corner, and I decided to ask them straight up about the tinkers. If they didn't know, who would?

"Excuse me, Officer," I asked. "What's the deal with the tinkers?"

"I wouldn't worry about them, sir," he said. "We'll be having two other guards down here in an hour. And we've been in touch with some other guard in the area, so I don't think we'll have any trouble at all."

With that, he crossed the street. A boy with his arm in a

sling had overheard what I had asked the cop, and he offered an opinion.

"The tinkers," he said, "I wouldn't fook with them."

I went back into the pub. There were two people there, a bartender and a youngish guy in a sort of rugby shirt and slacks. I sat down and ordered a Guinness and listened to their conversation. They were both local people. The young man, Kevin, commuted to Dublin, where he worked in construction. The old bartender's name was Sean. They were talking about the tinkers. Like so many other Irish people I'd met, they let me slip seamlessly into their conversation. I asked them who the tinkers were.

"They're outsiders," said Sean. "They've never really caught on."

"They don't have a home," Kevin said. "That's the big thing with them. They don't have a place. They take everything with them. Because they don't have a place, they don't respect anybody else's place."

I felt sorry for the tinkers, but I could see that sympathy wasn't the correct reaction.

Sean was proud to say that he never served tinkers. He said that a tinker once offered him a hundred pounds, but he still refused to serve him. Kevin found that difficult to believe.

"You'd serve a fucking monkey if he had a hundred pounds."

"Monkeys," said Sean, shaking his bald head, "but not tinkers."

But the tinkers were coming and it was time to shut down. Kevin said goodbye and left in a hurry. I walked to the door with Sean, who locked the pub door and stood outside, watching the street. Outside every store and pub, there was a man standing.

I walked up the street to Bridie Levins's place. I noticed I was walking pretty fast. I passed the boy with the sling. He looked at me.

"Don't fook with them," he said. I went home. Gary Cooper didn't have to deal with tinkers.

The tinkers are sometimes called "travelers." They are a very small minority in Ireland. No one knows for certain just how many tinkers exist in Ireland, but there are about twenty-five thousand. They are not just a loosely organized group of disenfranchised people. They have a language (sometimes called Gammon, Shelta, or simply "the Cant") and a distinct culture, and they have been around a long time, since the twelfth century, according to some sources.

"Tinkering" itself, repairing metal things like spoons and wheels, is not something you can make a living at in Ireland, so they do other things to get by. A lot of people, like the pub owner I talked to, don't even like to talk to tinkers. Ireland is one of the friendliest places on earth, but the tinker is a true pariah.

No one knows how exactly the tinkers started living the way they live. Some people told me that the tinkers are the descendants of people who lost their land during the potato famine.

They live on the road in encampments. There is no plumbing or electricity, of course, and most of them are constantly on the move. They are not above applying for public assistance, although some people told me that the government relief agencies have certain "tinker hours" when they will see these people. Even Irish people on the dole, it seems, don't like to be in the same room with tinkers.

This is, as you might figure, a very rough existence. It is estimated that 80 percent of the tinkers are less than twenty-five years of age.

I finally saw some tinkers when I was in Ireland. They were passing through on a country road outside Athlone and someone pointed them out to me. They looked very sad to me. There were a lot of children and one or two old men with white beards. I said, aloud, to no one in particular, "I feel sorry for them." The man I was standing next to looked shocked at my sentiments.

"Don't be sorry for them," he said. "They're the wrong ones for that."

Because Ireland has been "owned" by somebody else for much of its history, it may be that the unfortunate human quality of hating the oppressed group has never had a chance to get started. Whatever the cause, the Irish people as a whole are the friendliest people I've ever encountered.

I speak from a severely limited context. I grew up around Philadelphia, "The City of Brotherly Love." I have never had a moment in my life where I felt for even a nanosecond that "The City of Brotherly Love" didn't begin and end with quotation marks.

Because the first impressions of life form the background for what is to follow, I have always felt that I could say, no matter where I was, "This place is friendlier than Philadelphia."

Everyone has heard of Philadelphia's storied crabbiness. These stories are not apocryphal. When they had an Easter Egg hunt between games at a Phillies doubleheader, people really did boo the little kids who didn't find eggs. Mike Schmidt's nine-year-old son was, after the discovery of his identity, actually booed by the other kids at the schoolbus stop when his dad came to get him on a rainy day. A guy dressed like the Atlanta Falcons mascot was beaten senseless at a Monday night football game (afterward, an onlooker said, memorably, "He was asking for it").

I have my own minor horror stories. I asked a waiter for catsup and was asked "Why?" I once asked a guy at a Philly food stand, "Can I get a Coke?" I was told, "If you have money and you give it to me, yes, you can have a Coke."

Since my first impressions of the world were formed in the Philadelphia area, I tend to think, *These people are nicer than the people I'm used to.* No matter where I am (if, of course, I'm not in the greater Philadelphia area), I think that.

All of the time we were in Ireland we never saw any good old American rudeness. I saw a couple of loud drunken arguments, and they were curt with the tinkers, but, in general, everybody seemed to obey the rules of decency.

That's why it's too bad about England.

SEVEN

∼ *Unfortunately England* ∼

We drove south from the Cliffs of Moher and came upon a little town named Milltown Malbay. We decided to stop there because we wanted to get something to eat.

Milltown Malbay looks like a typical small Irish town (after we had seen our twentieth Irish town we realized that, on the surface, almost all little Irish towns look pretty similar). The stores are all freshly painted. (That is an actual local ordinance in many of the towns. If you own a little store you have to paint it every year.)

There is, in every little Irish town, the following: a pub, a drugstore, a grocery store, a couple of bed and breakfasts, and a Catholic church. The church is by far the most impressive building in the town.

We walked up and down the street and finally decided to visit the pub. This is an easy thing to decide in Ireland. We ordered two Guinnesses. I took a sip and was startled by how good it was. I buy Guinness in America once in a while, but I now realized that the brew doesn't make it across the ocean in its full glory.

I took another sip. Again, fabulous. I could see why Guinness had its position in Irish culture. It deserved it. But while I was in Ireland I discovered the dark side of the lovely brown liquid. I normally weigh a little over two hundred pounds. I'm a pretty big guy. I'm sixty-two and I weighed 190 in high school. I weighed myself the day before I left for Ireland. I weighed 200. With my Doctor Atkins Guinness diet, I gained a pound and a half every day. I discovered that I weighed 225 after seventeen days there. If I stayed in Ireland for six months straight, I could begin a new career in sumo.

When we were back in America we had planned to go down to the mouth of the Shannon and see Loop Head. It had a cool name, and there is supposed to be a legendary city there under the water. But if we went north we would be driving along Galway Bay, and we were told that was beautiful. So, we decided that we would just continue whichever way we were facing. This is a good method of Irish decision-making. Saint Patrick was supposedly buried at the spot a horse chose to stop. We didn't have a horse, so we went with the "whichever way we're facing" method, got into the Punta, and drove out of Milltown Malbay.

After about ten minutes we figured out that we were going north.

We looked at our map and decided that we should spend the night in a little coastal town named Clifden. The drive there was amazing. Galway Bay is one of the most beautiful areas in Ireland: mountains, streams, sheep, and cattle, and here and there, a guy cutting turf. It's like the Platonic ideal of "Irish." Every time we rounded a curve there was another painting in front of us. We just kept taking pictures, because the scenery became more and more amazing as we approached the town.

We were pretty beat, so we decided to spend the night outside Clifden. We parked at a bed and breakfast. There are many, many bed and breakfasts in Ireland, so many that there are several organizations and a rating system. Kathleen and Michael Conneely owned the one we stayed at. They were so friendly it seemed as if we were staying with a family instead of renting a room. This is the way to see Ireland. At the end of our trip, when we stayed in a Hilton in Dublin, it seemed as if we were back in America.

The people who own the bed and breakfast actually live

there, so your room might have a picture of their kids on the wall. The bed might creak a bit and the sink in the bathroom might be cracked, but it always seemed infinitely better than a room with a minibar and "modern art" on the walls and an array of little plastic vials, envelopes, and bottles in the bathroom.

After checking in with the Conneelys, we drove into Clifden with the sun settling into the Atlantic Ocean. It looked like the sort of thing you put at the end of a movie, and we thought this day was just about finished. We went to the pub and had a huge meal: mussels and lamb and several pint glasses. Suddenly it seemed too early to turn in.

We walked the streets of Clifden looking for loud and overt Irishness. We found it at E. J. Kings, a nice-sized pub filled with a lot of loud Irish people listening to loud Irish music while they drank Guinness and yelled occasionally in each other's ears.

The music sounded like what is called, in Georgia, "traditional country." As I drank, it sounded better and better.

Everyone was smoking and talking. I quit smoking a few years ago, but it is nearly impossible to stand around with a bunch of Irish people and not get in a conversation, and that leads (me at least) inevitably to butt-land. When the band was between sets we talked about Irish politics, American politics, Irish and American theater and movies, books, college, and even money.

Around one-thirty, the place was still packed. Something I asked changed the tone of a conversation I was having with a young guy from Clifden. I asked him about the town. He told me, but as he told me, his tone changed, and I discovered something that never completely leaves the Irish mind.

He told me that Clifden exported a lot of crops. Then his voice got a little more precise.

"They exported a *lot* of corn during the potato famine."

Those English

This wasn't an unusual conversation. As I went around in Ireland, I found that the wound in an Irish person's mind is there because of the neighbor across the Irish Sea. These are ancient wounds in the Irish psyche, but they are real, and, if the people I met in Ireland are representative, the many many years haven't healed them. To understand anything about Ireland, one has to be aware of England's role in the sad Irish story that never seems to end.

In the movie *Trainspotting*, a Scottish kid complains about "being colonized by wankers." The wankers were easy on Scotland. England is, to this day, the big black cloud of Irish history. Daniel O'Connell, in 1827, put the English thing this way:

"Accursed be the day . . . when invaders first touched our shores. They came to a nation famous for its love of learning, its piety, its heroism . . . [and] . . . doomed Ireland to seven hundred years of oppression."

Ireland has a long, sad history with England. Every Irish kid who reads about it becomes another Irish mind with a little ugly area marked "England." No matter how it is sliced it's pretty grim. Basically, for much of its history, Ireland has been England's little island of slaves.

This is an ancient beef. How far back can you go? America is struggling now with the idea of reparations for the descendants of slaves, but first, to be accurate, they'd have to take care of the Native Americans. In the "Ireland and England thing," you can go back to at least medieval times and find England mercilessly beating up on its neighbor island.

The basic ugly situation is this: England "colonized" Ireland by force, and created a woeful state of affairs wherein the Irish people who lived in Ireland didn't legally "own" their own country. The country was England's, and they "rented" it out to Ireland. Ireland "belonged" to England, basically, because England said so and England has a better army.

If Ireland were a building, this might have "worked." As Ireland is a country that was literally stolen from itself, it created quite a bit of what one Irishman called "collective cognitive dissonance," among other things.

These facts seem to be central to the Irish mind, at least the Irish mind as I've encountered it: England has caused great, unjustified, immoral, grievous, and totally unnecessary suffering to the people of Ireland, and has done this for centuries.

This is pretty much a given in the Irish consciousness. The widely circulated Irish *Notes for Teachers* calls the Irish "a race that has survived a millennium of grievous struggle and persecution." For a lot of Irish people, and a lot of Irish-Americans, that pretty well sums it up.

The Irish, as you might figure, didn't submit meekly to the English. There were dozens of rebellions small and large, but England always won, and Ireland went deeper into oppression. The pattern was oppression, rebellion, English victory followed by increased oppression, rebellion, and so forth. Rinse, repeat.

After every rebellion there were always those saying the equivalent of "Ireland's freedom must be watered with our blood in order to grow." There were always more Irishmen willing to die for the next unsuccessful rebellion.

Among first-generation Irish-Americans, my introduction to "British Studies" was typical. The first thing I remember my parents telling me about England was that England had treated their Old Country in a very cruel manner. I was about six when they first told me that. I didn't know anything about the "Old" Country; I didn't know where the "Old" Country was. How did it get to be "Old"? Do you wear out countries and then change them?

I didn't know the capital of the country was Dublin. I

thought, until my big brother straightened me out, that Ireland was a part of New Jersey. I knew nothing about Ireland, but I knew that the English guys were the bad guys.

There is an old joke that is so well-known in Ireland that you can't tell it because everyone has heard it. It's not a funny joke. It's a painful joke. Here it is:

God is in heaven. He seems to be very busy, and Saint Michael the Archangel comes up to him and asks him what he's doing.

"I'm making this little planet. It's called 'Earth.' Everything is going to be balanced there. There'll be North America and South America. North America will be rich and South America will be poor. On the whole planet everything is going to be balanced."

Saint Michael sees a little green dot in the Atlantic and asks God, "What's that?"

God says, "That's a little place called 'Ireland.' It's going to be the most beautiful place in the world. It's going to be very, very green, with lots of rivers and lakes and streams and little hills and mountains. And the people there are going to live in peace and harmony. And they are all going to be the people in the world who have the nicest life and the most beautiful land."

"How is that going to be balanced?"

"Wait till you see the neighbors I'm giving them."

This is, of course, a little rough on England. When I was growing up I would look at David Niven (who seemed to be in every movie when I was a kid) and think, "If they're all like this little guy with the mustache, they can't be that bad." And Cary Grant? He's English and I like him. Who wouldn't? This guy is charming and has a self-deprecating sense of humor and very good manners. How bad can he be?

If they are all people like David Niven and Cary Grant, why do my parents think that the English are monsters? By the time of *The Avengers,* with the beautiful Mrs. Peel and the funny Mr. Steed, I was pretty sure that England wasn't, as my dad put it, "a cesspool of iniquity."

But my dad had history on his side, and as I got older, the

more I read, the more angry I got at the land of Niven and Grant and Mrs. Peel. It is irrational to hold a grudge against an entire nation because of something done centuries ago. Still, when you read the history of English-Irish relations, you can see that the collective Irish mind is less than thrilled by England. In very compressed form, this is the sad history. When every new Irish schoolkid comes across it, another Irish mind is less than thrilled:

It is startling to discover that Ireland was first "given" to England by Pope Adrian IV, who officially handed it over to Henry II in 1155. (This is all the more startling when you consider how much Ireland has suffered because of its Catholicism. To the English way of thinking, Ireland "provoked" a lot of hostility by supporting Catholic causes throughout modern history. But if you want to put the blame on one guy, it's Pope Adrian.)

How did Pope Adrian "have" Ireland to "give"? Constantine was the Roman emperor who made Christianity the empire's official religion. According to something called the "Donation of Constantine," Constantine "gave" the Catholic Church a whole lot of countries, Ireland included. So the pope, the head of the Catholic Church, could give these countries to anyone he wanted. He "gave" Henry II the emerald isle in 1155.

Unfortunately, the Donation of Constantine later turned out to be a forgery. Everyone chose to ignore that fact. From 1155 on, the king of England "owned" Ireland. He could do what he wanted with it.

There were, however, some strings attached. The pope gave Henry the country under the stipulation that he would convert Ireland's hordes to Christianity. Since this was centuries after Saint Patrick, Ireland was already a Christian country. The pope apparently either didn't know or chose to ignore that. (Otherwise, why the stipulation? How could he not have known? He didn't get the paper that day?)

There was one other string. The pope asked Henry to require every Irish person to give the church a small amount of money.

Out of this simple seed, a monstrous tree grew.

Henry II didn't care much about Ireland. It was little, nearby, and comparatively peaceful. Right after Ireland was "given" to Henry, however, things got a lot less peaceful.

After the death of Brian Boru, there were a series of undistinguished kings. In the year the pope gave Ireland to England, a man named Rory O'Connor had the crown. A thoroughly loathsome Leinster man named Dermot MacMurrough wanted to topple O'Connor, but the Irish people hated MacMurrough, so he went to England and asked Henry to help him. Henry told him that he wouldn't send any men, but the Leinster man was free to ask any of Henry's noblemen.

MacMurrough convinced the earl of Pembroke, better known as Strongbow, to help him. Dermot offered him a lot of money (he even threw in his daughter!), and Strongbow said he would help him in Ireland.

Though MacMurrough had been beaten by O'Connor before, when Strongbow joined him they easily defeated the Irish. The Irish had very primitive weapons, and it was an easy, but vicious, victory. They started in Wexford on the southeastern coast and worked their way up, slaughtering Irish people on the way.

O'Connor read the handwriting on the wall and tried to make peace by offering old Dermot the crown if he would just stop the massacre. But it was no longer even an Irish war. Strongbow decided that he liked Ireland, and he wanted to be king. Henry II saw what was happening and paid Strongbow a visit. Strongbow didn't want to go up against the massive power of England, so he pledged his loyalty to the English crown.

Henry was happy with that, but in 1177, he named his son John "Lord of Ireland." A few years later, John became the king of England, and it was now official: The king of England was the king of Ireland as well.

Compared with most English monarchs, John wasn't that oppressive. He even did Ireland some good. He brought the English trial-by-jury system of justice to Ireland, and he minted coins (with harps), but he just wasn't that interested in Ireland. He let his noblemen run the place. They built and lived in the many castles that are still in Ireland, and they treated the Irish like inferiors, and they stole from them and cheated them. By and large, though, this was the benign era of English-Irish relations.

A lot of the English nobles left their castles empty and just went home to England. This would have been fine with the Irish, but the noblemen still owned everything. There were the infamous "absentee landlords."

In 1258 the Irish got fed up and proclaimed an Irish king, Brian O'Neill. As you might figure, England came over, crushed the rebellion, and took Brian O'Neill's head back with them.

Without war, Ireland started to develop a pretty prosperous economy. (This was during the era depicted in the Mel Gibson movie *Braveheart*.) England, under Edward I, started using Ireland's resources pretty heavily. Ireland was a good supplier of many commodities, but, to the English, the most valuable was soldiers, which the king used ruthlessly in his battle with Scotland. After Scotland "won" its freedom (the end of the movie *Braveheart*: They picked a good place to end, a subsequent history muddied up the Scottish "victory"), the Irish asked the Scots for help against England, but they were refused. (No one is going to make a movie out of this because the Scots and the Irish didn't get along well.)

Continued unrest in Ireland forced Edward III of England to enact an extreme "straighten up and fly right" edict called the "Statutes of Kilkenny" forbidding any interaction between English and Irish. The use of "Irish names" was forbidden. The Irish sport of hurling was forbidden, and even Irish music was against the law.

It was impossible to enforce these laws, but they did arouse even more Irish hostility against England. By the end of the fourteenth century Ireland was a kettle about to boil over. Irish chieftains had just about taken over the island. (Early in the fifteenth century Ireland actually had an Irish ruler again, James Butler.) The only solidly Anglo area was a little strip of land from Dublin to Drogheda called "The Pale."

Finally, in 1511, England spoke again. Henry VIII sent over a mass of troops. They had trouble with the native Irish fighters who knew the land so well, and they had difficulty establishing a final victory. In 1541, in a "declare victory and leave" gesture, Henry proclaimed that Ireland absolutely belonged to England and that was the end of it, so there, nyah, nyah.

Needless to say, it didn't "take." There were many Irish uprisings, and Henry's daughter, Elizabeth, sent English troops to control the Irish barbarians. Shane O'Neill, an Irish chieftain, was called before her in an effort to establish dialogue. He behaved very "Irish." O'Neill, when asked to speak, first howled like a wolf for several minutes and then spoke in Gaelic, which no one in Elizabeth's court understood.

The sixteenth century ended with a series of battles in Ireland. Sometimes the Irish won; sometimes the English. This was followed by the era of the most horrible Englishman of all: Oliver Cromwell.

Most Irish people think there is nothing in their history as horrible as the potato famine, but the Cromwell era comes pretty close. Cromwell was the Puritan leader who gained control of England in the 1640s. Cromwell was an Englishman who regarded the Irish as barbarians, but also as ungodly, which for Cromwell was much worse. Cromwell was a fanatical Calvinist Protestant who looked at Ireland as a sort of "Island of the Damned," and he acted accordingly.

Cromwell didn't, of course, exist in a vacuum. Puritan England's hatred for Ireland was widespread. Consider this extract from a Puritan pamphlet published in the middle of the seventeenth century: "These Irish, anciently called Anthropophagi (cannibals) have a tradition among them, that when the devil showed our Savior all the kingdoms of the earth and their glory he would not show him Ireland, but reserved it for himself. . . . They are the very offal of men, dregs of mankind, reproach of Christendom, the bots that crawl on the beast's tail."

The town of Drogheda lies on Ireland's east coast a few miles north of Dublin. Today it is primarily known as the town that Oliver Cromwell viciously destroyed. Today some historians try to depict this in a better light, but by all accounts, it was a horrifying massacre. Cromwell's army slaughtered at least a thousand men, women, and children.

Priests were burned alive in churches. This didn't bother the hyper-religious Cromwell because, as he wrote, "I am persuaded that this is a righteous judgment of God upon these barbarous wretches."

Cromwell was so brutal at Drogheda that other Irish towns started surrendering to him as soon as they heard what he did. Wexford, the exception, received the Drogheda treatment. Women and children were not spared. Cromwell left before he was finished, but his officers eventually completely crushed Ireland.

England treated the Irish as if their neighbors weren't quite human. England employed "mancatchers," who were paid by the head for rounding up stray Irish people. Women, especially young, breeding women, brought a higher price. The Irish were then herded into pens and branded. Then they were sold into slavery and sent to either the American colonies or the West Indies. Many were given names so that "they might thus lose their faith and all knowledge of their nationality."

It was very important to Cromwell that the Irish be defeated spiritually. He set about making every surviving Irish person convert to the Protestant side. Many did this to avoid being killed, but Cromwell never got the Irish "hearts and minds." In the West of Ireland a lot of the people "attending" Protestant services didn't even speak English.

But, on the surface, Ireland was a Protestant country. Protestants now owned all of the good Irish land. Eastern Catholic owners were forced to give up their good farming land and move to the stony west. Priests were hunted and killed. Going to mass could get you killed. Furtive Catholic services were held outside using large rocks for altars.

In all, about one-third of Catholic Ireland was killed during the horrible era.

Oliver Cromwell is not a popular man in Ireland. The very sound of his name evoked a reaction like a profanity in Ireland.

When he died, and Charles II became king, things got slightly better for Ireland. About a third of the stolen land was returned, but by and large, life in Ireland was still utterly miserable.

In 1685 James II, a Catholic, became king and tried to return Ireland to Catholicism. Back in England a group that wanted James's son-in-law, William of Orange, to become king, opposed him.

In 1690 James and his Irish partisans were defeated by William III in the most famous battle in Irish history, the Battle of the Boyne. England tried to make sure that there was no other Catholic uprising in Ireland, and they were utterly ruthless about it. This vast hostility was embodied as the infamous "Penal Code."

Catholics were barred from the army and the navy and every single civic activity. Catholics couldn't vote or hold any office. If a Catholic landowner died, and one of his sons was Protestant, that son got all the property. Catholics were not allowed to attend school. Turning in "renegade" Catholics was encouraged. All Catholic priests and Jesuits were banished from Ireland.

"The Penal Code," as these post–Battle of the Boyne laws were called, was described by the English statesman Edmund Burke as "a machine as well fitted for the oppression, impoverishment, and degradation of a people, and the debasement in them of human nature itself, as ever proceeded from the perverted imagination of man."

You would think that the Catholic religion would have faded away in Ireland, but it didn't happen. Ireland, throughout the saddest centuries, hung on to the Catholic faith. Despite prodigious efforts, England never subdued the Irish Catholic faith. Some call this miraculous, while others see it as part of the stubborn Irish national character.

The seventeenth century was very rough on the Irish. In 1649 Catholics legally owned 59 percent of Irish land; by 1714, the number was 7 percent. The Irish now had to pay rent on the land that had always been theirs. They had to support a church that was not theirs, a government that was not theirs.

Late in the eighteenth century, encouraged by the French and American revolutions, Ireland developed a grass-roots revolutionary movement, a group of Irish farmers called the Pikemen. They were named after the metal weapons they had forged. They were also known as the "United Irishmen."

By 1800, after massive carnage, England finally decided to make Ireland "part of England." It passed something called the "Act of Union." There were now Irish people in Parliament. The penal laws were abolished. In 1829 the Catholic Emancipation Act meant that even Catholics could serve in Parliament. Things seemed to be looking up.

But then just when it seemed that Ireland's long sorrow was ending, things got really, really bad. If God did this, wrote an Irishman of the 1840s, it was difficult to see just what he had in mind.

EIGHT

~ *Becoming a Tourist* ~

We noticed that we were hanging by the ocean, so we decided to venture inland. Mullingar was our destination. We knew some people, Americans, who were staying for a few months for business reasons. They were not at all unusual in this. All over Ireland you will find Americans who are engaged in a prolonged Irish stay for economic rather than recreational reasons. Some of these businesspeople fall in love with Ireland and want to stay permanently. An equal number (generalizing from my limited experience) want to get the hell out of Ireland as soon as possible.

The people who wanted to stay were people who were repulsed by the fast-paced thing that America circa 2000 has become. These people often expressed a sincere loathing for things like answering machines, impersonal, computer-generated "customer service," both-parents-working-strangers-raise-the-kids weeks, thirteen-hour workdays, and so forth. These people wanted to escape. In Ireland they thought, briefly, that they had found what they were seeking. However, once they stayed in Ireland, they found that Ireland (at least the eastern half of Ireland) is very much like the America they wanted to escape. Even in the west, you see things like a guy taking a break from farming to take a call on his cell phone in the middle of the field. I took a great picture of a sweaty, salt-of-the-earth guy in a field surrounded by sheep with a Nokia glued to his ear.

The Americans I know who hated Ireland inevitably complained about the things that the other Americans were vainly seeking (the sheep, the slowness, the bog, good water pressure in the shower, and so forth).

The truth is, both of these groups, in the long run, aren't going to like Ireland. The slow Ireland lovers need to look into the Robinson Crusoe/*Castaway*/Carlos Castaneda area. A smaller uninhabited island is what they seek. The slow Ireland haters already have what they want in America.

The really great thing that you can find in Ireland is very subtle. But it's over there. In Ireland aka God's Waiting Room. If you walk into an "Irish" store in America, you will find, on a coffee cup or a piece of linen or a T-shirt, some version of these words: *There are two types of people in the world—the Irish and the people who want to be Irish.*

That sounds a bit cocky, but after a few days of wandering around in the West of Ireland, I started, in a way, to believe it. But "Irish" doesn't have anything to do with the gene pool. "Irish" means something else. Many Americans (like Paulette and me) who spend enough time there begin to feel it. It happened to Paulette and me after about a week in Ireland, and it happened to almost everyone I talked to who had visited Ireland. It has to do with time. (I'm not going Stephen Hawking on you.)

In America everyone knows what time it is. They know how much time they have until they get to the next thing they're going to do. Life is a series of little hurdles. We see them coming. We anticipate them. We approach them. We go over them. Then we do the same thing again in a slightly different form. Some of the hurdles are higher than others. "Work" is pretty high. "School" can be pretty high. "Fun" is low. "Death," the last one, is a big Marine-style wall.

In Ireland there aren't any hurdles. You still have to do everything you have to do in America, but you don't run to hurdles, and you don't have to jump them. You can just walk around them if you feel like it. You get the overwhelming feeling: *This can all happen without me. Pretty soon it will.*

You don't dread leaving the stage, but you don't want to hurry it either. And, at any time, there's always time for a cup of whatever.

Mullingar has a bad-sounding name. I can imagine what James Joyce would do with that name. But it's actually a very nice place: sort of halfway between Mayo and Dublin, in every sense. Mullingar is usually considered a "market town." It's set in an area of beautiful peaks and valleys. The Irish type of peak and valley. Very gradual and not too shocking. Something to paint, not climb.

There are a lot of tiny lakes around Mullingar. All of this is "landscape by God" except for something called the Royal Canal. The Royal Canal was Irish made under the gentle guidance of the Brits, hence the name. The idea was to connect Dublin with the Shannon. This made a lot of sense in the eighteenth century because heavy things were then moved on water.

By the end of the nineteenth century, of course, the Royal Canal didn't have a raison d'être anymore, but it looks nice. Today the banks make a nice place for bicycles, and there are always a lot of them. The old canal is also, apparently (on the day we arrived, at least), big with fishermen. These fishermen, however, looked much more the Dick Cheney variety than the Saint Peter type. They looked like a Lands' End catalogue.

Mullingar has a beautiful Catholic church. Even among Irish Catholic churches, it's something. We spent about an hour in it. The hour seemed like five minutes. In a church, I really felt "the Irish Factor."

In Ireland I slowly noticed that I was responding to things in a different way. Everybody has had the experience of going on a vacation and taking off the watch and seriously slowing down, but in Ireland my experience was much different. I really felt that the old Frank Gannon was back there a couple of thousand miles away, while this Frank Gannon was a completely different person.

When talking with someone I started to respond in a very non-me way. I would pause a little before replying. I would savor the words I had just heard, and reply in a more measured, oblique way. I would think about every word I said and heard. I found that the "point" of the conversation was the least important part. I started to look at conversation as little dances. Sometimes I would follow, sometimes I would lead. But I gave up the idea of any kind of conversational destination. A conversation in America was a walk in a straight line. A conversation in Ireland was a meandering walk in the woods with lots of detours along the way. And I never thought much about where exactly it was going.

Rob Pelot is a guy I knew from America who was now living temporarily in Ireland. He was living, along with his wife Linda and their boy Kyle, in a nice hotel in Mullingar. Rob is an engineer and his company was, like a lot of American companies, establishing a base in tax-friendly Ireland. Rob, Kyle, and Linda were having a nice time, but Rob told me something about working in Ireland that clicked with my own Irish metamorphosis.

"The Irish people are great people to work with," Rob told me over a couple of Guinnesses in a pub in Mullingar, "but they have a very peculiar quality about them. We'll spend a couple of weeks working on something, some engineering project, and the Irish engineers are very good, very well-trained, but sometimes, we'll get to a little snag in something. This will be on something we've spent weeks on, and the Irish people will just look at each other and say, 'Oh well, I guess it's not going to work.' And that will be it. Maybe four or five weeks right down the drain. They are ready to ditch it just like that. Like it had no real meaning to them. Sometimes they are right. It's just not going to work. But an

American would sit there for a couple of hours before he gave up. The Irish guys seem like they get into the work that leads up to the project. But the final solution, they just don't give a shit about it."

The road is more interesting than the thing at the end of the road. And, after a couple of weeks in Ireland, I found that I had adopted that attitude. Commitments? Expectations? Goals? I gave up on all that and found that it wasn't missed. I existed in some little, tranquil, directionless state. There was no point in hurrying because where were you hurrying? There was no point in slowing down because why slow down? There was no point in stopping, unless, of course, you felt like it. We drove and we ate and we talked and we went to the bathroom. Our plan now was completely gone. Our modified plan was completely gone. The very idea of having a plan seemed absurd. What good can a plan do you in such an unplanned environment? No plan can help, so the answer seemed clear: Avoid all plans!

We neither reaped nor sowed, like the birds of the air. We slept when tired. We slept where it seemed good to sleep— on the ground, wherever. When I had to go to the bathroom, the bathroom became optional.

I once had a job as a security guard. I had only *one* duty: Turn on the lights. Yet I forgot this at least 25 percent of the time. I sat there in the dark like an idiot, until it finally hit me: I've *forgotten* something!

It was like that now in Ireland. I struggled to keep the only two ideas I had to keep: 1) In a couple of weeks we have to be at Dublin airport. 2) Find out where Mom and Dad came from.

Like the lights at the factory, these ideas kept leaving my brain. I finally wrote them on my hands: Dublin and Mom and Dad, in big red letters.

I started to think of my mental state as related somehow to Ireland. Despite the fact that I have always been an airhead, I think the Old Country contributed to my condition.

As I wandered around, I found myself doing odd things. Like watching turf-cutting. Turf-cutting is not a great spectator sport, but in Ireland I watched a lot of turf-cutting, and I was not alone. I watched a turf-cutter for over an hour one day. There was a crowd of about ten people with me. Some left, some came, but the crowd stayed about ten. Some brought food, which they shared. The tool that turf-cutters use, I learned, was a "slan." The turf-cutter we were watching was very good with his slan. The crowd actually made comments.

"He's good."

"Look at that!"

"Man can handle that slan."

That was about it as far as commentary went. You don't need Al Michaels and John Madden to call a turf-cutting.

I couldn't imagine killing an hour doing something like this in America. Even doughnut-making or taffy-pulling gets old in a hurry in America. But watching turf-cutting seemed like a fine thing to do in Ireland. Next time I go back, I'll know what to look for in slan handling.

Every night in Ireland we slept in somebody's house. There are bed and breakfasts all over the place. Many of them have a little green sign. The sign means that the tourist authority, the Bord Failte, has inspected them. The best thing about them for me was the odd sense that I was home. My mom's sense of what should go where is the same sense that informs all these B&Bs. Anne Forde, decorator, seemed to haunt the B&Bs.

Except for the brief time we spent in Dublin, somewhere in my mind, I was home. My days always began the same way. The B&Bs were all different, of course, but they sort of bled into each other and I find that I have one big memory of Plato's Irish B&Bs.

I open my eyes in a room that looks like my room. Not the

room I've been sleeping in for the past ten years. This room is like the room I slept in thirty-five years ago.

This room has one bed instead of two, and the wallpaper is different. Still, there are many similarities between this room and the room I slept in as a child.

There is a holy water font near the door so you can dip your finger and bless yourself when you enter. There are three crucifixes: one over the bed and one on each side. I find this very comforting somehow, as if I am, in some odd way, back home again.

I get out of bed and look at myself in the mirror. I see a guy with a beard and some gray hair. The guy in the mirror has wrinkles and squints like a man who wears glasses but doesn't have them on right now. He's only been in Ireland a few days and he is developing a Guinness waistline.

I'm in Ireland, not the New Jersey of my youth. It's July but the windows are a little fogged with the cold. I wipe the fog off and have a look. It's the Atlantic Ocean out there. I look over and see that Paulette is looking out the other window. We've only been awake for thirty seconds but we're already looking for Irish stuff.

After a low-water-pressure shower we get dressed and head downstairs for the breakfast portion of the bed and breakfast experience. I'm already looking forward to what I know will be downstairs.

"The Irish breakfast" that is served at B&Bs and hotels is a remarkable thing. The standard meal is this: a lightly fried egg, some homemade sausage, two kinds of bread, coffee and tea, sliced mushrooms, sliced tomatoes, Irish bacon, pancakes, ham, some fruit, and usually, another variety of homemade sausage.

This might have been more accurately titled "The Major Cardiac Event Breakfast." Anyway, people seemed to eat it and live. (I saw four people eat it and make it out of the room.) So, I, too, ate it. I could feel an artery closing as I took the last delicious bite.

We ate "The Irish Breakfast" every day we were there and made it back to America. I'm sure many were not that lucky.

As you eat your Irish breakfast, you will probably be joined by other visitors to Ireland. When we were there we met people from all over Europe, but most of the people we met were Americans. Many were just traveling around, but many were engaged in "searching for their roots."

Most of the Americans weren't first-generation Irish-Americans, but they had some Irish connection they were searching for. It is amazing how many Americans are of Irish ancestry. For instance, 30 percent of Massachusetts is Irish. As you might figure, that is the state with the highest level of Irish ancestry, but many other states are close. Rhode Island, 22 percent. Delaware, 21 percent. New Hampshire, Kentucky, and Tennessee, one-fifth Irish. New Jersey, my home, 18 percent Irish ancestry. If you put an "O'" or a "Mc" in front of many, many names, they sound quite Irish.

On this particular day, at this particular table outside Clifden, the people at the table with us are Mark and Marcie Berk of Philadelphia. They are very typical of the Americans visiting Ireland with some genealogical motivation. Marcie's family has the Irish connection. One of her grandparents emigrated from Ireland. She didn't know where her people came from but she was just trying to establish the general area. Mostly the Berks were having a lot of laughs. They had been hitting a few pubs, listening to a lot of Irish music, and, as happens to everyone who goes to Ireland, the beautiful places and the lovely people genuinely touched them. They would be back. They almost didn't want to find out too much about Marcie's ancestors. They wanted a reason to come back.

That was a very typical morning. If you went to Ireland in 2001, meeting and talking to Americans was something that came up all the time. Although some Americans attempted some form of camouflage, their Americanness was painfully obvious to the natives. As soon as you opened your mouth you screamed "American" with your "Yank accent." I grew up in an Irish home, but sometimes in Ireland people would be so struck by my manner of speech that they would say, "Say that again. That's lovely."

There were many other red flags.

Americans tip way too high. In Ireland bartenders and waiters get paid a decent wage, but they are very happy when Americans come in. It means tips that are uncalled-for, but welcome.

Americans call the money "punts." Although that is the official term, I rarely heard it used by Irish people. Pounds and pence are normal speak. The "euro," which I had read so much about, is rarely used, except in banks. (In 2002, I am told, this has changed somewhat.)

Irish tourism is a massive, billion-dollar industry, and the quest for Amero-Benjamins has taken some truly bizarre forms. One of the most appalling manifestations centers on the famous John Ford movie *The Quiet Man*.

The Quiet Man is a wonderful movie, but it has become, in America, the cinematic equivalent of watching a Saint Patrick's Day Parade while eating corned beef and cabbage and washing it down with green beer. The touristic essence of *The Quiet Man* is floating all over 2002 Ireland.

"*The Quiet Man* Experience" is an amazing commercial construction I observed near Castlebar. The movie is almost fifty years old, but still alive in the tourist mind. For a reasonable fee the tourist is given the opportunity to dress as the characters in the film ("The Colleen"[Maureen O'Hara]; "The Yank" [John Wayne]; "The Priest and the Minister" [Ward Bond and Barry Fitzgerald]; and "The Big Brother" [Victor McLaglen]) and be photographed in the act of acting like Irish people in a simulacrum of the little thatched cottage. The fortunate tourist will be able to (from the brochure) "get a feeling of what life in Cong was like during the filming by reading local newspaper articles of the time."

The brochure goes on to say, "Painstaking effort has ensured that all the furnishings, artifacts, costumes, etc. are authentic reproductions [a phrase Richard Nixon would love]. The four-poster bed and the tables and chairs which 'Mary Kate' cherished, the thatched roof, emerald green half door and white-washed front combine to enchant all who visit it."

I was assured that this is a popular attraction for tourists.

"We always have lines," the guy in front of the attraction told me.

One night in a pub, a young Irishman named Robbie Walsh told me something I remembered. Considering the time of night, that is worth mentioning.

"Will you get offended if I tell you something?" He had to almost yell this over the frantic fiddling.

I assured him I was not easily offended. I was several pints past the point at which almost nothing offended me.

"You Americans," he shook his head. This was hard for him to say. He went on after my blank eyes gave him the go-ahead.

"You Americans, don't be offended, but you Americans are really, really stupid."

"Why?" I asked. I was genuinely curious.

"Because we can take anything, put a fooking shamrock on it, and you'll buy it. I could wipe my ass with a towel and sell it to you because it's Irish. I could sell some Yanks used toilet paper and they'd take it home, frame it, and put it over the mantel. Then when their friends came over, they could say, 'See that? That's real Irish used toilet paper. It came directly from Ireland. That is authentic Irish shite from the Old Country.'"

I nodded. He went on, screaming into my ear.

"Why will you Yanks, who have the best technology, the most advanced stuff on the planet earth, the most money, the best schools, the best everything, why will you Yanks spend good money on this shite? I saw a man selling fooking *sticks! Sticks he picked up off the fooking ground!* He tied a goddamn piece of green ribbon around them and he was selling them to the tourists at the Cliffs of Moher for ten pounds! He called them 'Celtic ceremonial twigs' or some shite. But he was selling them to the American tourists. And they were *buying* them!"

I looked at his utterly bewildered, alarmingly red face. We both had a sip. He had something else to ask, some over-whelming question.

"What in God's name is wrong with you Americans?!"

He offered his ear. I leaned over.

"Drugs," I said.

When we were in Ireland, I had an odd conversation with Paulette.

"Why can't you be more like these people?" she asked. It was a genuine question.

"What do you mean, 'like these people?'" When in doubt I always lean on some variation of "define your terms."

"You know," she said, "Irish."

"I am Irish, my mom's from Mayo and Dad is from near Athlone." I have said that sentence many times, my creden-tials for the Irish guy's club.

"You're more New Jersey than Irish."

This was true. Still, I liked to think of myself as "Irish," not "New Jerseyan" (is there such a word?).

"Well, I've spent a lot more time in New Jersey."

"There's your problem," she said. "If you could get rid of the New Jersey you, you'd be a better person. Like these peo-ple."

"How do you know that?"

"I just do," she said. "It's obvious. Plus, I know you. New Jersey. Not Ireland. Obviously." People always say "it's obvi-ous" when it isn't at all obvious, at least to me.

She explained further.

"You have a core of Irishness. But the years and years of New Jersey have built up around you, like rust. Now it has to be scraped away. If you did that, you would be a good person."

"How," I asked, "do you 'scrape away' New Jersey?"

"I don't think you can."

"So I'm stuck being a bad, New Jersey person?"

After a moment of reflection she said, "Yes."

I silently promised myself, *I am going to scrape away New Jersey.*

Many Irish writers modify their use of quotation marks or get rid of them altogether. Molly Bloom's reverie in *Ulysses* is just the most well-known instance of this. Irish writers from Flann O'Brian to Roddy Doyle have abandoned the quotation mark. After a while in Ireland, I realized why this is so. Conversation doesn't seem like something that requires quotation marks. It just seems that a period may be needed, maybe, at the end.

I left my bed and breakfast and decided to buy a local paper. It felt that this might give me a better feel for things. It was a rainy day (big shock there) and the store was about a block away. When I got in there I decided that I would get some candy and a few other things, maybe a cigar.

The man behind the counter, a man about sixty with a bald head, big ears, and interested-looking eyes, said something to the other man in the store, a younger man with a cap and a jacket and a cigarette. It went like this.

They're working on the road again and they don't seem to be any different than they were the day before. It's a wonder that we pay these people. They stand around and we pay for it. That's the system. They're working under the ground. I think it's the pipes. Now, what are pipes doing under the road? You'd think they could put them under the ground. Then they wouldn't have to be tearing up the roads. It's some sort of sewer apparatus that they're hammering at. Why do they hammer when the work involves pipes? You turn pipes, you don't hammer at them, for Godsakes. Did you see them? Yes they were out there already. Already, they've been there for three hours. Drinking coffee. My son works for the city and he spends half his day drinking coffee. Why isn't it tea? I'll tell you why. Because there is just coffee that they use for these things. And they can't bring tea? Sure, they can bring their own tea but why bring it when the city has coffee? It's a small thing to bring tea, but why not let them pay for everything? My son doesn't bring tea. But he doesn't like tea anyway. He drinks water. And we know why he's drinking water in the morning. The Guinness. He loves Guinness. He drinks that enough. Is he still doing that? He's doing that and a lot of things don't you know? His mother is beside herself with all that. I say don't worry about it. He's young. He won't be young for long. That's right, let him do his thing, woman, they'll have him tied down soon enough. The women won't understand that. No they've got their ways. They think a man should be a saint. A saint. Sure. They're all like that. Sure my boy was one but now look at him. Yeah you have to say that, you have to let them. You're from America. I could tell by the way you look. You might as well announce it. God bless you, are you down the road, you and the missus? No children. That's the way. Do it when you can. You only live this one time. And it's over before you get started. I was, it seems that way yesterday and now look at me. Yeah, look at you. Ah, you'll look like us soon enough.

Where do I put the quotation marks?

One of the really great things about Ireland is pretty subtle. When you are in Ireland you get, every day and free, the sound of "Irish English." I grew up listening to it, and I never get tired of it. People of the non-Irish variety have told me that they love the sound of Irish English. There is nothing like it, don't you know?

On the surface, one might understand why the Irish people might have a resistance to English, the language of their long-term oppressors. But that isn't the way it is. That isn't the way it is at all.

While I was in Ireland I tried to investigate the subject. What was there about the Irish use of English that made it such a wonderful literary tool? John Synge, the great playwright, said that whenever he was stuck for a line, he would listen to the western Irish people in the kitchen below his workroom. They would always give him amazing little tidbits like this one from Synge's *Playboy of the Western World:*

Christy: "It's that you'd say surely if you seen him and he after drinking for weeks, rising up in the red dawn, or before it maybe, and going out into the yard as naked as an ash tree in the moon of May, and shying clods against the visage of the stars till he'd put the fear of death into the banbhs and the screeching sows."

There were many times in Ireland, not always in a pub, when I'd hear amazing words put together in a way I had never heard before. While I listened to these little spontaneous prose poems, I would always think, "I wish I had a tape recorder," or, failing that, a much better memory.

These amazing little verbal flourishes weren't spouting from some poet or writer. Often they'd be coming from a guy who worked on the road or a bartender or just somebody who wandered in to sip a few. It's a place where words are important, where words, in a sense, *are* life.

The Mecca of all this Irish talk is, of course, the Blarney Stone. The stone itself is set in Blarney Castle in County Cork. The kissing of the stone is supposed to magically produce that "Irish talk" quality in the kisser. According to legend, Queen Elizabeth I was putting a lot of pressure on the local Blarney chieftain, a man named Cormac McCarthy (maybe a distant relative of today's Cormac McCarthy). Elizabeth kept pressing him for a tangible show of loyalty, and Cormac kept adroitly fending her off with a torrent of words. Finally, fed up with McCarthy's continual verbosity, Elizabeth is said to have screamed, "Blarney! Blarney! It's all Blarney!"

Since records of all the utterances didn't exist until the 1800s, the whole story is pretty dubious. But it makes for "some fine talk."

Whatever the truth, if you want to kiss the stone, which is located on one of the castle's parapets, you have to hang down and trust someone to hang on to your feet. (For the record: I did it; Paulette chickened out. Hey, I'm the writer.)

Cork

Cork is the extreme southwest of Ireland, maybe three car hours from Dublin, ninety minutes from the Cliffs of Moher. It's a small trip when you consider the fact that you'll be receiving the gift of eloquence. It will be more than handy if I'm ever audited by the IRS.

My mom and dad spoke "Irish English": That is, they spoke with a "brogue." The word "brogue" is Irish for "shoe," and it was originally used in a derogatory way, something like "having a shoe on the tongue." The shoes on my particular tongue are more New Jersey than Irish. The only trace of "brogue" in my speech is a tendency (I am told) to turn "th" into "d" once in a while. After kissing the Blarney Stone I expected that I would never again say "this" when I meant "dis."

Blarney Castle itself would be pretty amazing in say, Anaheim. But in Ireland, where castles are as common as lawyers in Jersey, it's not that striking. It's a nice enough castle, I guess. The most interesting thing about it is a bit of folklore/legend.

Supposedly a great many Irish soldiers escaped through a secret tunnel during the Cromwell siege of the seventeenth century. I would be very happy if that actually happened, and I can't say that it didn't. But it seems that whenever things get truly awful in human history, humans like to invent ways out. Someone escaped. Somebody got away.

Still, it's a pretty nice castle. It's a tower, actually. The towers always seemed to outlive the castles, much like all the antebellum chimneys in the American South that are all that is left of the old mansions. The chimneys stand out there alone in the middle of vast fields. There are a lot of solitary towers in Ireland. It's as if God wanted people to remember what was once there, and he left the tower to show you how big it was.

That explanation was given to me by an old man in Donegal. The more I think about it, the better it sounds.

One day I took a long walk in Ireland.

I got up from our B&B bed in Clifden. Paulette was asleep, so I took a shower and headed out. Taking a shower in your average Irish B&B is like standing naked, with soap, in the rain. It gets the job done, though. It just takes longer than you are used to.

I put on some khakis, some white socks, sneakers, a white T-shirt, a golf shirt, a sweater, and a tweedy-looking coat. I looked at myself. An Irishman out for a stretch of the leg. As I walked along I wondered whether anybody could tell I was a "Yank." I resolved to try out my pseudo-Irish accent on the first person I met.

I decided to wander along in a random fashion, always careful to keep the Atlantic Ocean on my right. I calculated that this must be south. I did this because of my complete absence of a sense of direction. I walked out of the little town and went happily on my way. I'm an Irish guy, I thought.

It was a cloudy day. There were a lot of birds. I walked for about ten minutes and did not meet a single Irishman or Irishwoman on my way. I didn't even meet any Yanks. It was a slow day for stretching the leg. I tried to think of Irish songs. I tried to think of that song that my dad used to play.

My brain did not cooperate. I ran through a lot of Smokey Robinson, a lot of Stones. Nothing Irish was stored up there.

I then saw someone approaching. An Irish guy. A wandering Irishman. As he got closer I could make him out. Tweed coat. Jeans. Big brown shoes with thick soles. He had a beard and a hat. A baseball hat. We got closer and closer. I could finally make out the hat. Boston Red Sox.

We walked up to each other and stopped. He spoke.

"Hey, how you doing?"

He sounded foreign. His accent was not like my accent. I spoke.

"Doin' good," I said.

"Where you from?"

"New Jersey," I said. It just slipped out. Damn. "How 'bout you?"

"Boston," he said. Now I knew the origin of this foreigner.

His name was Lynch. He was an internist. His people were from near Wicklow. He had been in Ireland for three weeks. He was staying the whole summer. His wife was Italian. He met her in North Carolina. He went to medical school at Duke. He said he had just come from Wicklow.

"Guess the name of the town we stayed at last night," he said. He had a big grin.

"Istanbul," I said.

"No," he said, "not even close. Hollywood." He started laughing. He had one of those laughs that makes you start laughing. I started laughing too.

We talked for a while. Our subject was Ireland in general. We agreed on many things. You can't get a good sandwich here, but breakfast, that's something. If we ate like this for long we would die. He then asked me if I had felt "the Irish thing." I said I think so. He said "the Irish thing" had several identifiable symptoms. It makes you talk in a slower, more roundabout way. It makes you feel as if you belong here even though you've never been here. Finally, it makes you feel that life is very wonderful but very temporary.

Yes, I assured him, I had felt the Irish thing. We said our goodbyes.

I walked until I saw a sign telling me it was eight miles to Screeb. I turned around. By the time I got back to Clifden, Paulette was waking up. While she got dressed I told her of the Irish internist I had met on the road to Screeb.

In Ireland, there are almost as many castles as there are big rocks. The first one I saw astounded me, but there are so many of them in Ireland that you start to get used to them. After spending several days at Disney World, you get sick of the "Magic Kingdom."

I read somewhere that Ireland has more castles and golf courses, per acre, than anywhere else in the world. I have reservations about the golf course claim (Myrtle Beach?), but the castle thing is undoubtedly true. They are all over the place and they usually have English-sounding names. So every time you look around in Ireland there's a giant house silently screaming, "England screwed us."

Some of these places are now tourist hotels. A few are private residences again. Dot-com guys and other rich people own them. Writers (very successful ones—J. P. Donleavy owns one; that Lord of the Dance guy probably does) own a few, and more than a few castles are still owned by the ancestors of the British people who had them built. These people are called the Anglo-Irish. They've been in Ireland so long they are more Irish than English.

A lot of the castles have tours, and we went on a couple of them. Most of the castles were built in the time between the Norman invasion and Oliver Cromwell's friendly tour. Most of the older castles are impossible to date because the records were destroyed in one uprising or another. Historians dated a lot of the Irish castles by finding similar structures in England. There's a lot of guesswork.

Norman-era castle life wasn't really all that lavish. "Living in a castle" was pretty tough. The castles were difficult to heat, windowless, and the bathrooms were built right into the walls. There was no plumbing, so it must have smelled terrible all the time.

By the time of Cromwell, things had improved a bit, but it still wasn't what you usually think when someone says "castle." A lot of the castles have a very tangled history with many owners, Irish and English, depending on who was running the general Irish show. But, if you go on a tour of one of these castles, it's difficult not to get the creepy feeling that the whole massive structure is just a giant reminder of English oppression.

The tour guide usually avoids certain awkward facts. Here is an all-purpose castle tour history:

Muck Castle

Lord Muck was visiting some of his money and one day he just happened to be passing through Gaelic Lough when he "fell in love" with the place. He ordered his driver to stop and said, "I will build a house right over there next to that cow."

He built this house as a charming understated place to go in the early to late spring. He had a large family and they needed a large house. That's what they got because there are twelve thousand tons of marble involved in the structure. Ten laborers died while building the house, and there is an old legend that their spirits inhabit the house, which is convenient because their bodies are embedded in the plasterwork and floor of the west verandah. On a cold fall night, they are said to wander the halls. Tourists sleeping at the castle have been known to complain about them!

Lord Muck married a girl named Madeline Blight-Ashen and she apparently loved gardening, or rather she enjoyed looking at gardening. In the major garden, there are several rare flowers that only bloom once, for ten minutes, every year. Madame bought enough of them so at least one in the crowd is blooming at all times!

I can't recommend these tours, but it might be "just the thing" if you are visiting Ireland, have some spare time, and want to look at a big, big house and feel appalled and revolted after lunch one lazy afternoon.

Later, back in a bed and breakfast, I thought about what Robbie Walsh had told me about Americans wanting to buy any little piece of Ireland, about them paying stupid money for stupid stuff. I thought about it, and it didn't sound so grotesque, so pathetic. It didn't seem like the gross stupidity it had seemed in the pub that night. Now, in the semi-glare of sunlight, it seemed almost touching. Irish people in America, most of them second- or third- or eighth-generation, know that they are Irish because people have always told them that they sound Irish. That's all they have of their Irishness. There isn't one tangible thing from the Old Country. They have no "Irish traits." They wouldn't be able to identify them if they had. Under the circumstances, paying twenty bucks for a pile of twigs from Ireland really doesn't sound bad. The long-lost son cherishing some fragment from his long-gone past.

I lay in my bed and looked out the window and thought, *It's good to be a tourist.*

Now, of course, we were tourists. Like it or not, that's what we were, two Yanks on holiday. I consoled myself with this thought: Sure, I'm a tourist, but my mom and dad were born here, so I am, after all is said and done, 100 percent Irish. I just had the misfortune of being born in America. In reality, the blood of Ossian flows through my veins!

I abandoned that thought. To paraphrase a good Englishman: He thinks too much. Such men are a pain in the ass.

We said our goodbyes to the real Irish people and the tourists and walked outside. The sky was as clear as it ever gets in Ireland. We were ready to go rambling. We knew that later, when we were going to track down my mom and dad, we would have a definite purpose and a definite destination. But for now we could go anywhere. We walked around talking about where we might go. We were within driving distances of many, many intriguing places: Bunratty Castle, the ring of mountains they call the Twelve Bens, the beach of Old Head. We had read and been told about these places that we could go. The Punta was filled with petrol and, after the breakfast, we had enough carbohydrates to drive to Africa.

"How are you feeling?" I asked Paulette. She was looking up at some sea birds flying overhead. In Ireland you look up a lot.

"I am feeling great," she said. "How about you?"

I said I was up for anything.

We consulted a little guidebook that we had brought. It had a lot of maps in it. The wind turned the pages so we had to duck inside the B&B. Paulette looked at the book. She had assumed the role of navigator. I looked out over the ocean. You could hear the waves. I started to think that the time was right to do something epic.

"Let's find God," I said.

I said it as a joke. But, after a minute, it seemed like a good idea. We knew that this was one of his favorite places. He was hanging around here someplace.

We decided to go to a place where he had been seen—if not God, at least his mother. That is a place in County Mayo called Knock.

Supernatural phenomena don't seem that weird in Ireland, for some reason. You don't hear two farmers talking in a pub about spirits appearing and statues moving every day, but the general atmosphere is a lot different than in America. In America, unexplained phenomena like that turn up in the pages of *Weekly World News*. America is filled with people who have had coffee with the postdeath Elvis when they weren't having sex with aliens, but you just don't walk around telling your neighbors about the statue who stole your dog. You don't want to be one of those people; you just know that they're around somewhere. In Ireland, these stories are taken differently.

"We listen to things with a carefully withheld incredulity," was what a distinguished older gent in Athlone told me. That seems to be precisely the Irish attitude toward weird stories. I'm listening, the attitude says, but you don't believe I'm buying this, do you? Nevertheless, I'll play along.

If you drive up the coast from Clifden toward Louisburgh, then head inland, you can get to Knock in a couple of hours. If Knock isn't the holiest place in Ireland, it's close. The little town of Knock is in County Mayo. Mayo is a rustic area and Knock is in the most rustic part of the country. Only one extraordinary thing has ever happened in Knock, but it was very remarkable indeed. On the evening of August 21, 1879, at the peak of the famine, a little girl looked at the southern gable of her parish church, the Church of Saint John the Baptist, and saw what she thought were statues of a woman and two men. She thought they had been newly placed because she hadn't seen them before, and she was a devout Catholic who went to church often.

What she saw weren't newly placed statues. The woman "statue" was a vision of Mary, the mother of Jesus. On either side of Mary stood Saint Joseph, her husband, and Saint John, the author of the last Gospel. To their right was a plain altar on which stood a lamb. Behind the lamb there was a large cross. Angels hovered around the lamb.

Fourteen other people reported seeing the same thing. Two ecclesiastical commissions investigated. After considerable examination of the witnesses and the site, the commission found that "the testimony of the witnesses, taken as a whole, was trustworthy and satisfactory."

Their conclusions permitted the establishment of Knock, like Lourdes, as an official holy place and a site for "Marian" pilgrimages. The Knock Shrine Committee was set up in 1935, and a folk museum was built at Knock in 1973.

Today there is a huge church where the little girl saw the apparition of Mary. Near it, there is a vast basilica. Near that there is the museum, which tells the story of the miracle of Knock, along with a sort of capsule view of rural Irish life through the past few centuries.

Although Lourdes is the more celebrated miracle, Knock is a vital part of the worldwide growth in devotion to the Virgin Mary in the twentieth century. In Ireland it was a big part of what was called "the devotional revolution," a sort of re-establishment of a direct emotional response between Ireland's Catholics and their faith.

I knew about Knock when I was a little boy because my mother told me about it many times. My mom, who grew up near Knock, had a little white book of prayers that she read silently, at the kitchen table in our house, every night of her life. When she went on vacation she brought the book with her. I looked at the book closely when I was a kid. There was a "Prayer for People in Purgatory," a "Prayer for People Who Don't Believe in God," a "Prayer for the Dying," a "Prayer for Sinners," a "Prayer for People Who Mock Religious Faith." A prayer for everybody.

My mom, unlike my dad, who was a voracious reader, never, as far as I know, read anything other than that book. You would see her looking at a newspaper or a magazine every once in a while, but you never see her reading another book. One time I asked her why.

She looked at me as if I had asked a question that had a very obvious answer. Then she said something I always remember.

Me: Why is that the only book you read?

Mom: What else is there?

When they are saying mass at the church at Knock, the priest's words are amplified and sent to the huge speakers they have mounted around the church and basilica. So no matter where you are in the town, you can hear the mass. I watched a guy pumping gas while around him I heard:

> *Lamb of God*
> *Who takes away the sins of the world*
> *Have mercy on us.*

Later, I saw a man outside drinking a Guinness and eating some dry roasted peanuts while this was in the air.

> *May the peace of the Lord be with you always*
> *Let us now share a sign of that peace.*

I looked over at a fat guy having some sausages at the table next to me. We nodded at each other. I wished the fat guy peace and he did the same, I guess, to me.

Knock has had a long-standing, Lourdeslike reputation for cures, and the sick and the crippled visit the shrine every day. When you walk around in Knock you are likely to come across a man or woman walking with a cane or a metal walker, head down, whispering the words of the Our Father or the Hail Mary or some private prayer of their own composition. It is impossible to spend any time in Knock and not feel the presence of . . . something.

Ireland has always had a particular love of Mary, the mother of Jesus. My sister is named Mary, and in an Irish phone book the first name "Mary" in front of a last name like Kennedy or O'Brian will take up a page or two. To use the phone book to call Mary Kelly of Dublin is a life's work.

A few years ago Mary appeared in Ireland again, in 1985. In a little village in Cork named Ballinspittle there is a little shrine with a statue of Mary. The shrine itself is not unusual. Irish people often have a shrine to Mary in the backyard or nearby. If you drive randomly through the Irish countryside the odds are good that you will encounter a shrine to Mary on the side of the road. We passed several of these driving around in the west when we weren't looking for them. When we saw a particularly striking one, we got out of the Punta to investigate. Some of the shrines are amazing things with painstakingly erected steps and kneelers and carefully planted flowers of all sorts.

But in 1985 a particular statue of Mary started to move. This movement was witnessed by at least ten people. When news of this appeared in the papers, some Irish wise asses drove around putting little signs on Mary statues with messages like INSERT COIN HERE and OUT OF ORDER.

But other people took the moving statue very seriously. Many interpreted the animated Mary as a sign of Mary's displeasure at something topical. Mary's appearance was attributed to whatever axe was being ground. Some op-ed pieces said Mary was appearing now because of abortions in America. Others said it was a sign of Mary's pleasure at something the pope said or the recent peace efforts in Northern Ireland. More than a few said Mary's appearance was an authentic miracle, but it was Mary herself attempting to help tourism. These observers seem to embody the sacred and profane in a particularly Irish way.

At any rate, crowds started to gather. Many more people saw the statue move. Some said that Jesus himself had appeared next to it. Some said that they saw the recently canonized Padre Pio, the Italian mystic who experienced stigmata, standing right next to Mary. He was moving around too. Wise guys speculated about the possibility of dancing. Does God like disco?

All of this filtered through the collective Irish mind and produced a lot of jokes. Some were funny. Some were sacrilegious. Some were funny and sacrilegious. The whole thing kept picking up momentum. All around Ireland a *lot* of statues of Mary in countless roadside grottoes started walking and talking and doing other things. There were stories in the paper of fervent atheists who saw what was happening and changed their minds in a hurry. A statue of Mary walking around and talking to you can do that to you.

The sleepy little village of Ballinspittle was on the map big-time. They ran charter buses to it. Tourist dollars were made by the grateful Irish merchants of the area.

But the summer passed, the tourists went home, and the statues stopped moving. Whatever you make of all this, Mary had grown even closer to the Irish heart, while doing her part for the vital Irish tourism industry.

My uncle John told a story many times in my presence. He performed it more than he told it. His voice would get very intense but quiet. The people around him would lean in to hear him, and he would tell his magical story of the wonders of Ireland:

"Way out in the West of Ireland, out in Mayo, there's this little winding country road. Just a dirt road really. You can hardly get a car down it; you may as well walk. You follow this road deep into the woods until you get to this amazing thing. It's a homemade shrine. There are rows and rows of rocks carefully placed. They're made into steps, and at the top of the steps there's a beautiful statue of Mary. It's all breathtaking and lovely but there's something really amazing about it. It's something no one has ever been able to explain. Scientists have been there, but everyone is utterly puzzled. The mystery is in that statue. Because no matter how long you sit there and stare at it—if you sit for days—no matter how many hours you stare at it, it never, ever moves."

I heard a strange expression in Ireland: "thin place." I asked an old man to explain it to me. He looked at me as if it were a hard thing to explain, but he would try.

There's this world and the next world. Some people call the next world Heaven or Hell, but no one who is in this world has ever been there, so no one can say what it's like there. It's just the next world. The door is shut and you can't see what's behind the door. Ireland is filled with very religious people, but no one knows exactly what "the next world" is like; they just know that it is there. That's the faith.

But there are certain places on earth that are closer to the next world. There aren't many places like that. But in these places, you are much closer to the next world than you normally are. You are so close to the next world that you can feel it: You can sense it. You can't quite see it, but it's very, very close. You close your eyes and you're almost there. A "thin place" is a place that is very, very close to the next world. Ireland is filled with little spots they call "thin places."

He mentioned some places in Ireland, but for me (and I think a lot of other visiting Americans), Ireland itself is one large, extremely thin place.

I'm not a very spiritual person. My mom was an extremely spiritual person, but I just didn't get that gene. I like to think of myself as a rational being. I am not a fan of *The X Files*. Watching the *Ghostbusters* movies with my son when he was little is as close as I've gotten to anything "paranormal." Nothing that I couldn't explain physically has ever happened to me. I've never believed anybody who told me about UFOs or channeling or past lives. I don't even believe Shirley MacLaine exists.

But I know what that old man was talking about. Ireland. The thin place. That's a big part of why people are drawn to it even though the food stinks, it rains all the time, there aren't any beaches, and driving around can be "Death Ride 2000."

They go because it's the thin place.

In Ireland there are "official" thin places all over the countryside. If you walk down a path in the West of Ireland, chances are you'll run into a genuine thin place.

Late in July every year thousands of people climb up Patrick's Mountain in County Mayo. The climbing day is called "Reek Sunday." Some years over thirty thousand people make the climb. We didn't have that many when Paulette and I gave it a shot.

Patrick's Mountain is no Mount Everest. The Irish "mountain" is only about twenty-five hundred feet high. Still, it is, as they say, a good stretch of the leg. Thousands make the climb every year because, it is said, at the top of Croagh Patrick there is a bona fide thin place.

The climb begins at dawn, and people start arriving well before sunrise. The round trip up and back takes about four hours. But people are always eager to make the journey. There's a chapel at the top of Croagh Patrick. It's a certified thin place, and a lot of people see the whole arduous journey as a spiritual as well as physical experience.

Paulette and I took the trip to the thin place. It wasn't easy. There were lots of falls, and I ripped a kneehole in my pants. It took almost three hours to get up there, but the place was, as advertised, a genuine thin place. How do I know that? You try it and then tell me. There is a little chapel at the top, but even if there was nothing up there but rock, I believe I still would have had the thin place experience.

But that wasn't the only thin place we encountered.

All the time we were in Ireland, we felt the same thing. I couldn't define it, but it was there. And, as soon as I got back to America, it vanished. When I returned to America and got off the plane at LaGuardia, as I walked to the luggage pick-up I saw a little lady who seemed to be in her seventies. She walked up to a large man. He was wearing clothes that identified him as an airport employee.

"Excuse me," the old lady said, "I need to talk to somebody who can help me."

The guy walked away. "Find one," he called back to the lady.

At that moment I knew I was back. Back to the thick world.

*　　*　　*

The "otherworldliness" of Ireland also makes death seem much closer. I am in my forties. I like to think I have a lot of life coming to me, but in Ireland I was acutely aware how brief life is, how tentative our hold on this world is. I remember Yeats talking to an old Irish woman. I remember what she said.

"In this life all you have is a mouthful of air."

I never felt that way in America. In America death, like almost everything else, is easy to ignore. In America death is like a flute player in the last row of the orchestra. You can just barely hear him back there. In Ireland, however, death always seemed to be sitting next to me with a program in his hand. In the "thin country" death lives across the field from you in his little white house.

The Irish personification of death takes many forms: A banshee is a woman who comes wailing from the sky to take your soul away because you are about to die. When you are dead you will be placed in an open coffin while the people who knew you when you were alive stand around drinking and talking, and half of their conversation is directed toward you. The Irish people that stayed in Ireland throughout the nineteenth and twentieth centuries have not only accepted death; they've gotten used to him. He's the bad guest who will never leave. We know he's here but we'll ignore him. We'll talk around him, but we can't quite forget that he's here.

He was here a long time before Saint Patrick. In the evening the wind would rise and the door would be barred and he would sit there next to the fire. When you walk at night in Ireland he's all over the place. In Ireland they have what they call *celi*. These are places for neighbors to gather. They go there and talk about what has happened, but it doesn't sound like something that really happened in the real world, but it did happen. The telling of it makes it sound like a fairy story, which it is, but it's also the way things are in Ireland, the place where things are different. Is it more real or less real? I can't say. I can only say that Ireland is in the thin place.

*   *   *

Ireland has always been a country characterized by deeply held beliefs. Over 90 percent of the people are Catholic, but the Irish people believe in many things that are not outlined in the Baltimore Catechism.

An Irish poet once told a story of walking around in the West of Ireland talking to the peasants. One particular conversation was with an old peasant woman. This was in the 1920s, but I think you could have the same conversation today, if you tried hard enough. It went something like this:

Irish poet: Do you believe in heaven and hell?

Peasant woman: No, of course not. Heaven and hell are just something the priests made up to scare you.

Irish poet: Do you believe in God?

Peasant woman: The big man in the sky? No. That's something for children.

Irish poet: What do you think happens to you after you die?

Peasant woman: You go into the ground, you rot, and that's it.

Irish poet: Do you believe in the fairies?

Peasant woman: Of course.

While we were in Mayo, I felt that it was a good idea to discuss something very close to the Irish heart: fairies. We were seated around a large table at a pub called the Weir House. Several glasses had been emptied. It was a large happy table. Tongues were loosened, and the fairies crept into the conversation.

The fairies turned out to be a very good subject for round table discussion. Almost everyone had something to say about the fairies. In some areas, it was well agreed that fairies, whatever else they do, generally do five or six things.

One of the characteristic fairy activities involves marriage. If you married a beautiful woman, it seemed, the fairies came and took her away on your wedding night. This was a pretty well-established practice. So, it seemed, all of the married women in Ireland who were, after all, still around, not stolen away on their wedding night, just didn't make the fairy-take cut. There was a lot of discussion. Perhaps, a very judicious man named David offered, the fairies' standards of beauty are much different than the humans'. Therefore, a very beautiful woman, by all human standards, might nevertheless be left behind. David is a counselor.

"Obviously," he said looking around the room, "that's what has happened here." He smiled and took a well-earned sip of Guinness.

David, I thought, is a very wise Irishman.

I had never heard the term "fairy fort" until I was in Ireland. People around the table were using it as if "fairy fort" were a day-to-day word. I had to plead ignorance, and I was told that a fairy fort is a raised circular mound of earth surrounded by bushes.

"Does nature naturally form them?" I asked.

"Fairies naturally form them," I was told, as if I were the slow student in Fairies 101.

There is a lot of action in fairy forts. If you're standing outside near a fairy fort, you can hear the fairies busily going about their business. No human has ever been inside one of these things, but everyone at the table except Paulette and me had stood outside listening. Fairies are really noisy. If you don't bother them, they won't bother you, generally speaking. I had adopted the "suspension of incredulity" look by now, and no one stopped talking to look at me anymore. The collective discourse on fairies continued.

These fairy forts are taken seriously by the government, which has given them protective status. A house builder named Tommy had actually been forced to move a planned house because it "compromised" a fairy fort location. These things were taken seriously. Paulette and I also took them seriously for the rest of the evening, which was several hours.

The next day we were taken to an actual fairy fort. I didn't see any fairies. This was a fairy fort that was newly constructed. I looked around for tiny lunch pails. No luck. Back home in New Jersey the first question would be: Do fairies belong to a union? Then they would see if the fairy fort were up to code.

There was a house twenty feet away. It wouldn't bother the fairies over there. You don't want to bother them. They are touchy and vindictive. But that's just their nature.

It might seem odd, at first glance, that the most Catholic country in the world persists in these odd old beliefs, but after I thought about it for a while, it all seemed to make perfect sense.

I have spent a lot of time in big Catholic suburban churches in America, and I never got any kind of sense of collective belief or any kind of spiritual sense at all from the people standing around me. I felt that the center of the service, the part that everyone was focused on, was almost always the collection. And the second collection. And the brief third collection right near the end.

I used to joke with my sister that her big Catholic, suburban New Jersey church with "interesting" architecture should be called "Our Lady of the Property Values." If it didn't have a sign outside, you would never think it was a church. It looked like a planetarium.

I couldn't imagine getting on my knees and praying in that church. It would be like kneeling in the frozen food section of Kroger. But in Ireland, in every little town we went to, we would walk around, check out the standard pub/B&B/chemist/produce line of freshly painted store fronts, and then we would walk over to the church. It was always open. We would go inside and kneel. It seemed the natural thing to do.

In Ireland, more than anyplace else I've ever been, the people have not lost their souls. This has to do with a lot of factors, a lot of history. But I think a lot of it has to do with just the place itself, the natural state of Ireland.

In Ireland, I was reminded of something I read in an

American history course in college: Seealth, chief of the Squamish, talking about nature. *The natural world is sacred.*

You have to fall in love with Eriu, "the most beautiful woman in the world," and she's right outside the door. The spiritual world is the real world. And the real world is the home of the fairies.

I learned a lot about fairies that night in the Weir House. The fairies are very fond of mushrooms. They use the mushrooms mostly, it seems, as furniture. Fairies are all very different, but the one thing they do not like, the one thing they really frown on, is someone who doesn't believe in them. That guy, the nonbeliever, is in for serious trouble, a hard road, a tough lot. Pity him, because he'll suffer, that one.

A very pervasive fairy activity is stealing babies. A fairy will come into the nursery at night and steal the baby. This fairy story stands in for the truth—the high infant mortality rate in rural Ireland. Fairies, it seems, are more apt to steal male babies. That's why very young Irish males wear dresses. So fairies can't tell they are boys.

There are fairy stories in virtually every country in Europe, but the Irish fairies seem unique in that they have quite individual traits and personalities. Alfred Nutt, who wrote widely on the subject, believed that each locality in Ireland had certain very specific rituals associated with farming and agriculture. So it seemed natural to give the fairies associated with one area distinctive traits.

The two types of fairies that seem to be distributed all over Ireland were the banshees and, of course, the leprechauns.

The banshees have escaped America's schlock machine, but the poor leprechaun has been captured by America and forced to appear on cereal boxes and in those horrible movies, which are so bad that they keep making sequels. My son has *Leprechaun in the Hood* on DVD. That fills my heart with joy.

"Leprechaun" comes from the word "Lu-chorpan," or "Wee Bodies." The leprechauns in ancient stories are shoemakers. If you capture them, they will tell you where their crock of gold is hidden, but leprechauns are pathological liars, and they are very deceptive. As a result, no one ever finds the gold.

The banshees don't have a trade or a home. Their only function seems to be to appear when someone is about to die. Banshees are selective, however. They only show up when a person with a Gaelic name is about to die.

I did not get out of Ireland without an encounter with the fairies.

One night as I walked back to my bed and breakfast near Spanish Point, I got close to the fairies. It was a cold night, and the sea air was gusting. I had to walk through some trees because they were working on the road and you had to take a little detour. So, not thinking of what might await me, I walked into the dark Irish woods. I am a boy from Camden, New Jersey, and I am not at home in the woods, even for just a couple of minutes, but it wasn't very far. (For the record, I had consumed two [2] pints that evening, far below the level where I begin hallucinating.)

I stepped carefully. This was thick wood, and I could only see a few feet right ahead of me. There was a little meandering path that seemed to go where I wanted to go. It was very quiet in the woods. But not completely quiet. You could hear something. The light from the moon shone through the branches and you could see the individual leaves as they caught the light. They seemed very, uh . . . vivid. Somewhere inside me a little voice said, *This is getting a little weird. And you're not reading a Stephen King novel.*

I made my way through the woods. It was only a couple of hundred yards, but I am very bad on directions, and I started to doubt myself. Was I still going the right way? The voice in my head got harsh. I could see myself getting lost in the damn Irish woods. Two hundred yards and the American idiot gets lost. I could hear my mother's voice: *"God save us, he'd lose his head if it wasn't screwed on."*

I used the moon as a direction finder, but it still seemed

like a long two (or was it three?) hundred yards. It seemed like a mile and a half, maybe. I tried not to feel that I was getting lost, but it was getting difficult to avoid that thought.

I began to sense that I was not alone. There was someone near. I could sense it. It was like when you know there's someone at the door before he knocks. So you open the door and there he is with his fist raised to rap on the door. That happens all the time. Now it was happening in Ireland, but there was no door. Just stupid Irish trees.

I almost called out, "Hello, is anyone there?" but I stopped myself. How big a moron could I be? People might be walking by and hear me. Then they would come see if I was hurt. I'd be standing here in all my stupid big American glory. I did not need that scene.

But what was it? Whose presence was I feeling? I said to myself that if there was an animal, it could not be a dangerous animal. Maybe a rabbit. Or a deer. Was I afraid of Bambi, now?

I made my way along. As I walked along carefully, a thought came into my mind and stayed there. It stayed there until I finally saw my bed and breakfast.

I believe in fairies. Leave me alone.

As I nodded off to sleep, I held that thought.

I took several moonlit walks after that. Sometimes alone, sometimes with Paulette. There was always something out there. Waiting.

If you go into the woods at night in Ireland, don't go alone. Because you won't be. In Ireland no one knows what "Augh!" means.

There are fairy stories that explain and comment on everything that there is in life in Ireland. The symbols of Ireland—the harp and the shamrock—are spiritual symbols, and it is impossible to think of a nonspiritual Ireland, a place entirely bound by the laws of physics. The Irish are "the ancient dreaming race." When I think about Ireland, I think of it as a place where there are fairies all over and they aren't going anywhere. They're in the woods.

I've never had anything like a religious experience. Whenever anyone says that he had one, I think of Ray Robinson and George Foreman.

Sugar Ray Robinson had one after he collapsed in the 102-degree heat at Yankee Stadium against Joey Maxim. He said he saw God in his locker room after the fight. George Foreman after losing to Jimmy Young saw something similar. Indians who want to see God don't drink any liquid for four days. A dehydrated brain is close to God. For me, it's also close to Dumbo.

God has never come up to me and pinched me. He's never come to me in a dream like the Old Testament guys. When I was in college I read William James and I put the God experience in the box labeled "discharging lesions of the occipital cortex." I don't know what that means, but when I say it people look at me as if I know what I'm talking about. Boy, are they deluded.

Everything that happened in my life happened because somebody caused it to happen and I could, in many instances, name the person who did it. My unfaith has been around a long time. It started when I was twelve or so.

I used to do magic tricks when I was a kid. I did one that was great. Not David Blaine great, but better than you would expect from a kid doing tricks for his parents and friends in his dining room. This was the great trick. When I was twelve.

I first got a dollar bill from a subject in the audience. I had my assistant write the serial number on a handy blackboard. Then I took the dollar, rolled it in my hands, and made it vanish. (I'm not finished. I told you it was great.)

My assistant brought in a tray (a "TV dinner table," as it was called). I selected someone from the vast audience (ten if I was lucky). There were five oranges on the tray. I asked the chosen party to select one. She did. I asked her to slice it open (supplying the knife). There was a dollar bill tightly rolled in the orange. I asked her to unroll it. I asked her to read the serial number. Yes, indeed, a match! The same number that was on the dollar the guy gave me! Thank you very much. No, I can't tell you how I did it. A magician never tells.

One day, I did tell. There are two dollars. The number is subtly changed. I "force" the girl to pick the right orange. The dollar goes up my sleeve. It's all a trick.

After I revealed the secret, nobody liked it. It got around.

In Ireland nobody tells. Because nobody knows. There is no place like Ireland. It is a place where the Stone Age is literally still there, but they have cable TV and cell phones. You drive past little towns with churches too big for the towns. You pass weird stone structures erected long ago to weird old Druid gods. Everywhere there is the other world rubbing right up against this world.

There is a world with weird old gods who steal children and leave their doubles. (The Irish had the mystical equivalent of cloning a long time before Crick and Watson.) This is a world where screaming spirit women take you to the land of the dead. This is a land where the most important building in town is the Catholic church, but it's built within sight of a pile of giant stones erected in honor of some huge ancient deity.

In this land, the spiritual realm is very real, and you can't even ignore it if you want to.

In the magazine of America "Religion" is a very small section. You flip through it quickly. There's not much to it. It reduces itself down to a box you check when you apply for some things. Catholic. Jewish. Protestant. Other.

"Hey, they're getting pretty personal here." But you go ahead and check the box next to "Catholic" or "Jew" or "Lutheran" or "Episcopal" or "Presbyterian" or "Evangelical" or "None." You don't like to check "None." What are you, a troubled loner? Get with the program. Which place did your parents take you? Put that. Don't cause trouble.

It's the magic conversation ender. If you say, "Barb and I

are Lutherans," the guy who asked you will say, "Do you go to First Lutheran?" and you say, "No. We hit the Second Lutheran." Then the guy says, "Ah," and it's time to change subjects.

Religion is like "I have a bad case of halitosis" as a conversation ender. There is nothing you can say about your religion or your halitosis that anyone really wants to hear about. They'd rather listen to Conelrad on the radio. They'd rather read cereal boxes.

But go to Ireland; spend some time and, voila! everything is different. "Religion" there *really* isn't a subject. They *never* talk about it. But it's not a subject for discussion because it's not separate from life. While I was in Ireland I tried to think of what that state of mind was like and I came up with this: It's the same state of mind you had when you were ten years old. When you are ten you don't know anything. When you are forty, you know a whole bunch of things but you don't know why you're here or where you're going. If you're going anywhere.

There are worse things. I found that I was an Irish Catholic the way I had two arms. That was the way it was. Period.

There are worse things.

Because Ireland is the land where the next world seems so close, the place where the ghosts in the machine take a coffee break, it seems a huge contrast to America, where the Disney Corporation produces all spirituality. The one thing that underlines this more than anything else is an Irish saint's feast day, Saint Patrick's. The American Saint Patrick's Day and the Irish Saint Patrick's Day are, well, oceans apart.

Every year on March 17, America becomes conscious of the Irishness in its midst. That is the one day every year that allows people to wear garish green clothing and say things like "Sure and begorrah." People wear pins that say things like "Kiss me, I'm Irish." Restaurants serve corned beef and cabbage. A lot of bagpipes are heard. Some people dress as leprechauns. They are usually drunk when they do this. There are big parades in New York, Boston, Chicago, and, surprisingly, Savannah, Georgia. Food coloring is added to malt beverages. It is, for those who are Irish in America, all pretty repulsive. Someone writes an op-ed piece about how repulsive it is. The op-ed piece is repulsive.

Saint Patrick's Day in America has an odd history. The earliest Irish immigrants were from Northern Ireland, Protestants from Ulster. Their early marches and celebrations in America were a celebration of the Battle of the Boyne, the 1690 battle in Ireland where William III, a Protestant, defeated King James II, a Catholic. Saint Patrick's Day, first celebrated in the middle 1800s in America, was a counter-demonstration by later Irish Catholic immigrants, a sort of in-your-face to the Protestants. Saint Patrick's Day today has virtually nothing to do with any of this, but that's how the celebration started in America.

On Saint Patrick's Day in northern Georgia, where I now live, hardly anything unusual happens at all. Some of the bars have green beer specials, a particularly nauseating practice. On TV, they show the episode from *Bonanza* where Hoss sees little men dressed in green and assumes they are "what they call them there, leper-cons, Paw! I seen 'em, Paw! You gotta believe me!" Nobody believes old Hoss and his face gets mighty red. The rest of the show consists of the increasingly excited Hoss seeing the "leper-cons" and rushing to get Paw or Little Joe (Adam had, I believe, already said *"adios"* by the time this epic episode was made). Of course the leper-cons always disappear right before Hoss gets back with a witness. As a result, Paw and Little Joe begin to assume that Hoss has been involved in substance abuse.

The background music for this episode is truly remarkable. David Rose and his orchestra (who had an actual chart record, "The Stripper") play the most grotesquely "Irish" music I have ever heard, music that perfectly evokes the "pseudo-Irish" experience.

The Saint Patrick's Day *Bonanza* episode. See it!

On the last few Saint Patrick's Days, I have established a little ritual. I have a little dinner with a few friends. I play Chieftains records. I try, yet again, to make soda bread that doesn't taste like papier-mâché.

It's not a big deal at my house. Paulette isn't Irish, so my kids are only half Irish. I tell them about my mom and dad a little, but it is all pretty remote. I am sure that my kids will not think of themselves as "Irish." They will say, I think I'm half Irish on my father's side.

Things were different when I was a kid. As soon as I say that to my son, I feel as if I am an official old coot.

But things *were* different.

My parents would mark March 17 on the calendar. They would talk about it as if it were Christmas. "Only three days!" my mom would say. When the big day was finally here, we would get all dressed up and go out to my cousin's restaurant for the Saint Patrick's Day Hibernian celebration. We would sit around a big table in a room with many big tables. We had dinner. Then the MC would introduce a priest or, rarely, an actual monsignor, to say a prayer. Then a speaker would be introduced. I saw many speakers, but in my mind's eye, I always remember the speaker as a fat guy with a red face and a carnation.

I remember not "getting" any of the jokes. I'm sure they weren't dirty but they were "over my head." They involved mothers-in-law and mortgages and doctors and priests and rabbis. The Irish people around me laughed at the jokes. As the speech went on, and the amount of consumed alcohol grew, they laughed louder and longer. By the end of the speech the speaker was doing very well, getting big laughs.

After the speaker, the band started playing. They always started with an Irish song or two. "When Irish Eyes Are Smiling," played up-tempo, was a popular opening, but they soon went into non-Irish music. Cole Porter, other standards, and "songs you only hear at wedding receptions."

At first there would be only one or two couples dancing.

Then, as the drinking continued, the floor would fill up. There would be old people dancing with young people, women dancing with women. Everything was permissible, except, of course, two men dancing together. Please, this is a saint's day here.

There would always be one or two little girls there who were about my age. At a certain point my mother would try to induce me to dance. I remember going into the bathroom and staying in there for about an hour to avoid this sort of thing. I would come back from the bathroom and stop at the door to the ballroom. I would peek out and see if my mother was still seated. If she was, I would return to the bathroom and count things. I would count tiles, cracks, anything. Then I would return to my post outside the ballroom. I would peer in again. If my mother was dancing, and therefore unable to press me into dancing, I would return.

I remember these evenings as incredibly long and tedious, but I was internally very happy, so I never complained. I knew that I, unlike my non-Irish friends, didn't have to go to school tomorrow.

It is easy to forget that Saint Patrick was a real historical figure. For the Irish, he was the man who forever changed the entire country of Ireland. He changed it spiritually and socially. In Ireland, that's almost everything.

He did this by absorbing the old Irish pagan ideas and making them cohere with Christianity. No man ever succeeded at anything more fully. Ireland has remained overwhelmingly Christian and Catholic despite enormous obstacles, and it may remain that way forever.

Saint Patrick, whatever legends are associated with him, was real, and we know more about him than we know about most people of this era. Even if all of the myths about him are false, Saint Patrick still had an amazingly singular life. He was, in the real sense of the words, the mysterious thing called a holy man.

Patrick first came to Ireland against his will. He was kidnapped from Britain and made a slave at the age of sixteen. He tried to make the best of it in his assigned role, herding cattle. He learned the language, the people's customs, and, most important, their pagan religion. Patrick, however, remained a steadfast Christian who prayed for hours every day. He wrote that he said over one hundred prayers a day and felt the presence of the Christian God all around him. There was in Ireland an ancient prophecy of a man who was to come and "destroy our gods." Patrick turned out to be that man.

If Patrick was the man, it means, of course, that the pagan's scriptures were right. So the pagan scriptures correctly forecast the coming of a man who would prove the falseness of pagan scriptures. The story of Saint Patrick combines the pagan and the Christian traditions in a remarkable way. When Patrick battles the magical forces of paganism he uses the magical powers of Christianity. Patrick wins, but the pagans put up a creditable fight. They go down swinging. Saint Patrick doesn't say the pagan ways were all bad. They were the old way; I'll give you the new way.

The most crucial thing that Christianity brought to Ireland was the written word. During the "Dark Ages" that followed Patrick, when Western civilization was in chaos, Irish monks kept the most profound ideas and values, the things that continue to be the bedrock of all civilization, alive and well. The fall of Rome brought on massive destruction. Irish monks were one of the few sources of classical learning.

The old Celtic civilization was actively hostile to the idea of writing. Things were learned by memory, and they were transmitted, to a select few, orally. There is an ancient Irish written language called Ogham, but it was very limited and could never be used to transmit anything complex. Christianity brought literacy.

Saint Patrick has such a strong hold on the Irish spirit that the Irish tend to forget all the other missionaries who aided in bringing Christianity to Ireland. A reasonable argument can be made that Christianity had a foothold in Ireland *before*

Patrick's return. And things were not so clean-cut. The conversion was very gradual. A lot of people held to their old pagan ideas and more than a few seem to have put up a lot of resistance. People being the way people are, some people probably died heroically in the cause of the old pagan way. But pagans were illiterate. Unlike their Christian counterparts, the pagans had nobody recording tragic stories of pagans dying for their faith.

One of the most amazing things about Patrick was the way he converted the noblemen of Ireland to Christianity. The peasants were becoming Christians all over Europe at this time. Peasants' lives were so difficult that they were very receptive to the message of Christianity and its promise of a new, better life after death. But the Irish nobleman's status, power, and influence were tied to his position as a high priest of paganism. Even the "disinterested lawyers," the Brehons, were threatened by Christianity because the religion brought its own sense of morality. In practice, Christian morality often undermined the Brehons' supposedly objective judgment. Once one side has God's favor, it's hard to win an argument. Most important, no Christian can ever be totally "disinterested." For the people of influence in Ireland's system, Christianity was a huge threat.

Despite this, Patrick was able to convert the very people Christianity threatened. I asked an Irish priest about the mystery of Patrick's conversions. How did he manage to convert people to Catholicism when Catholicism itself lessened their power, prestige, and money?

"God," he said. Good answer.

Whatever happened, Ireland was largely Catholic just thirty years after Patrick's return. Patrick established monasteries and schools, and the faith and a high degree of classical learning now walked hand in hand. During this period, Ireland was truly the intellectual center of the Western world. Thomas Cahill's wonderful book, *How the Irish Saved Civilization*, is not misleadingly titled. If you equate civilization with classical learning, Ireland *did* save civilization in the Western world. Without the work of the Irish monks, the work of Plato and Aristotle (along with many more ancient Greeks and Romans) would have been lost. It would have been a devastating blow to Western civilization.

Although Patrick himself wasn't a great scholar (his Latin, for instance, was very shaky), he completely changed the way learning took place in Ireland. In changing a pagan oral tradition into a Christian written tradition, Ireland became, as the nuns told us, "The Land of Saints and Scholars."

Saint Patrick is certainly the main figure in the weaving together of pagan and Christian Ireland, but there was also another huge figure who is rarely mentioned, Saint Columba, the "Dove of the Church." Saint Columba, like Saint Patrick, was a real historical figure and we know quite a bit about his life. His biographer, Adamnan, depicts him as a man passionately dedicated to both learning and religion. Columba had a privileged background. Unlike Patrick (to the horror of every Hibernian, Patrick was a Briton), Columba was a native of Ireland. He was actually born as someone eligible to become the king at Tara, but amazingly he gave that up and pursued a religious life.

Columba was a quintessential Irish type, a holy man who would, after spiritual musings, punch you in the mouth if he felt you needed it. His prayer book is titled *Fighting One*. He was a great appreciator of the "old ways." The Irish, even though they became overwhelmingly Catholic, hung on to a lot of old traditional, "pagan" things. Columba, although a devout Catholic, seems to have been very sympathetic to certain aspects of pagan life. Although Ireland was by then an essentially Christian land, there were a great number of vestiges of the old pagan ways that were still part of the culture. "Fili," pagan poets whose role was, for the Irish language–loving people, spiritual, coexisted with the new church in Ireland, and Columba, despite Rome's ever-present authority, didn't see anything wrong with it. If the Irish want a little paganism with their Christianity, so be it.

Like Patrick, Columba knew the old ways very well. He was educated in a bardic school, and he stayed on friendly terms with poets his whole life, and when he died, a poet, not a bishop, composed his eulogy. Ireland had presented him a great opportunity to be an "Exile for Christ," a holy man who lives among "strangers" because he has abandoned his past life, a life among his peers, in his journey toward Christ.

Exiles for Christ

In the Irish countryside one can still find the little solitary cells that men like Saint Columba inhabited. Holy men, men who removed themselves from the world and helped establish the Catholic Church in Ireland, lived in these cells. They were called "exiles for Christ."

If you walk into one of these today, it is easy to imagine what men like Patrick and Columba felt. They had chosen to spend their whole lives in these little cells, isolated from friends, family, the world. Considering these men, I had an overpowering feeling of the transitory, brief nature of human life. Ireland was becoming, for me, a sort of "God's waiting room." I wasn't hurrying death, but I was aware of it as I had never been. I thought of some lines I hadn't thought about since college, from Yeats:

> *A man awaits his end*
> *Dreading and hoping all*

In Ireland the spiritual always seemed very close. I realized that I hadn't thought anything about my own death since I was a kid. Ireland didn't take me away somewhere; it just brought me home. I seemed to be unable to think without thinking of "the big picture." I was now thinking Irish.

*　　*　　*

For the Irish, literacy was almost equivalent to religion. From the beginning, the idea of learning was completely intertwined with religion in Ireland. The leading intellectuals were all monks, and the advanced schools shared their names with monasteries. On the surface Ireland's collective consciousness was now Christian. But a little bit of the "old ways" still hung on. The Catholic Church as an institution was, of course, centered in Rome. But you never get a sense that the early Roman Church somehow interposed itself in Ireland. Despite the formalities and dogma and rituals of a very organized hierarchical Catholic Church, Christianity in Ireland was a quite distinct thing. No one would have a hard time distinguishing between "Irish Catholicism" and "Roman Catholicism." In Columba's life and writings, you can see that calling the Catholic Church in Ireland "the Irish Church" was not a big stretch.

But the Church in Ireland was still the same Latin-based religion with precise strictures, and the Irish bishops kept the "Roman rules" in a hard-nosed fashion. The ritual and dogma stayed almost precisely the same as in Rome. The dates for feast days were slightly different (owing to the Irish adherence to tradition and a spirited defense of "the Irish Way" by Irish bishops, notably Columbanus, who butted heads, quite successfully, with Pope Gregory the Great).

In the early Catholic Church, there was a real fear of classical learning. The entire liturgy was written in Latin, the language of Nero and Commodus, and there is, throughout the Irish clerical writing of the era, an oft-stated warning, a great fear of somehow being swayed toward pagan ways. Since the early Irish Church hung on to a lot of pagan trappings, maybe the fear was well founded.

You find writings warning of "the temptation of grammar and the lure of Apollo." But in Ireland, the monks seem to have taken to Latin in a very serendipitous way. They played around with it. Latin was a language and the Irish have always seen words as playthings. Many see in the work of the early Irish monks the characteristic "Irish" quality. Even in a very solemn context, the monks found it hard to pass up an opportunity for a little laugh, a little wordplay.

I remember the first time I read anything "religious." It was the Baltimore Catechism. Almost immediately, I remember making up sacriligious jokes, trying to get a laugh out of the girl next to me. I hadn't realized that I was just doing what comes naturally to an Irish person.

During Columba's era in Western culture, when the barbarians went inside the gate, made themselves at home, and redecorated, Ireland became, for a while, the intellectual center of the Western world. In Ireland there was an oasis, a place where words mattered. A place where words were loved and coddled and cherished and fooled around with.

Because Ireland was the center of learning, students from all over Europe went to school there. The Irish monasteries also sent traveling scholars all over Europe. By the ninth century Irish scholars were famous throughout the Western world. Many countries had an Irish "visiting intellect" in their government.

For a while their great kings were saying, "Wait a minute. Let me ask the Irish guy."

Back home in Ireland the Roman Catholic Church started to have problems. The system was very detail-oriented, and this was impossible in Ireland, a land of very "creative" Catholics. Also, the Roman Catholic Church sent out trained bishops and assigned them to be the absolute religious power in that particular area.

The Roman system really had no chance of success in Ireland. Since people lived miles apart, the idea of a local bishop in charge of a particular area could never possibly work. If the ultimate arbiter is fifty miles away you don't consult the ultimate arbiter if you need a fast answer. You get creative.

So the monasteries became little self-contained areas, little cities, in a way. This is amazing when you consider that people who had the original impulse to completely remove themselves from society started these minisocieties.

The seed of these monasteries was always one Irishman who, driven by a spiritual impulse, completely removed himself from society because of a spiritual impulse. Such men were called "white martyrs." They were still alive, but they were "dead" to society. They had chosen to live, and die, completely alone. Now they found themselves surrounded by people who had similar ideas.

So these solitary cells all over the countryside often became monasteries. There might be one single hermit to join the original exile. Then two other guys who rejected secular life would join. Then a dozen. Pretty soon large groups started to live the solitary life. Paradoxically, hermits lived together.

This wasn't just an Irish phenomenon. The pattern was repeated all over Western Europe, but it seems particularly prevalent in Ireland. Oddly, Ireland started to become a powerful force in many other areas after the fall of the Western Roman Empire. Militarily, as well as intellectually, Ireland was a power. For a while, Ireland actually colonized parts of England. These isolated colonies were mostly in Wales and Cornwall. Cormac, an Irish scholar/bishop, wrote of this era: "The power of the Irish over the Britons was great, and they had divided Britain between them into estates . . . and they were in that control for a long time."

I, along with a lot of Irish people, like hearing that.

By the 800s Irish learning was well-established and respected and admired throughout Europe. This might have continued, but the Irish were actually riding a streak of what was for them phenomenally good luck. They hadn't been invaded in centuries, and the "invasions" often resembled unwelcome weekend visitors, more than the massive carnage usually associated with the word "invaded." Some call this Ireland's "Golden Age."

It changed, of course.

The first invaders were Vikings, and they did the usual sack-ing, pillaging, and raping. Although the Vikings never really succeeded in "conquering" Ireland, they did destroy a great deal of the carefully preserved writing of Ireland's great period. The nonmilitaristic (compared to the Vikings!), poorly organized Irish didn't have a chance against the invaders, and the Vikings pretty much did what they wanted to do. They slaughtered the Irish and destroyed their homes and public buildings. What they didn't destroy, they took back to Scandinavia. Today, historians have to rely on non-Irish sources to piece together a picture of what is left of "the Golden Age."

Vikings certainly killed a lot of Irish people and destroyed invaluable writings. Viking raids went on until 842, when the Irish and Vikings made an uneasy alliance. This didn't last long. The tenth century in Ireland was basically one big raid by the Norsemen, who looked on treaties as "suggestions."

The Viking influence on the little island wasn't completely negative. A lot of the larger cities (Waterford, Dublin) were established by Vikings. They established a coin-based economy, which was a big advance from Ireland's bizarre, cattle-based economy.

Still, there is an ancient Irish prayer that says it all compactly: "From the fury of the Norsemen deliver us."

But by 1002, Ireland, always a country of hundreds of autonomous tribes, had what some historians call its first real king, Brian Boru. He achieved this, largely, by being the first to even seriously consider the idea that one man could rule the whole of the island. There are many legends about Boru. They all emphasize two sides of his personality. He was a truly vicious warrior who could cut a man in half with one swipe of his sword, but he was, at home, a sensitive, poetic type who loved to play the harp and compose love songs. The two sides of Brian Boru are still pretty much the two sides of the idealized Irishman. He is always something like a "warrior/poet." The greatest Irish writing, I think, is similarly hard to pigeonhole. It is always profoundly "tragicomic."

After Boru's death, there were others who tried to be sole

ruler, but Boru was certainly the first. In *Darby O'Gill and the Little People,* Boru is the Man.

Brian Boru was very aware of the power of Christianity among the people of Ireland. He made his brother abbot of Killaloe, Holy Island, and Terryglass. He threw a lot of money at the Church and it bought him a lot of goodwill among the people and the clergy. This practice is still a good idea in 2002.

Today, there are actually some doggedly Irish people who attempt to trace their genealogy back to Boru. Every Irish kid knows who Brain Boru was, and he's achieved Santa Claus-like status. Mythic details have attached themselves to his life. His death is also rather myth-influenced.

The story goes that Boru died as an old man, but not in bed. He was watching a battle outside Dublin, and a guy from the other side crept up on him and killed him. The guy who killed him got his later, purportedly dying a painful horrible death. (I'll spare you the details, but his death made Mel Gibson's disemboweling death in *Braveheart* look like euthanasia.) Ancient Irish people weren't big on torture. They were big on *describing* torture. So the guy who killed Brian Boru (traditionally named Brodar) probably just got beheaded or something semihumane. For the Irish, unlike a lot of ancient people, executions were not long, drawn out, "Let's bring lunch!" affairs. For the most part, they executed quickly, by ancient standards.

Ireland has had a very violent past. It deserves a peaceful future and, as I write this, that may finally be the reality. An Irish peace has to be the best peace in the world. It's been a long time.

NINE

~ *What Are You Doing for Potatoes?* ~

During the potato famine, I was told, when someone asked you where in Ireland you were from, and you answered, "County Mayo," the person would respond, automatically, "God Bless You." ("It was like sneezing," a dark-humored Mayo man in his seventies told me one night.)

Mayo is the poorest county in Ireland, which, until recently, was pretty damn poor. The unluckiest people in Irish history wound up owning land in Mayo, which supposedly was too rocky and irregular for any major farming. The place seems like one vast contradiction: Its amazing beauty has been the stage for a history of appalling suffering.

"This is the only place that ever suffered because of one miserable tuber," my landlady told me right before we walked out to our car near the beginning of our trip. That thought stayed with me for the rest of our stay in Ireland. I spent a lot of time in Ireland contemplating potatoes. They're hard to ignore. They were at the table in some form for every meal we ate.

Since we were in County Mayo, not that far from the "Mom" area of part two of our journey, we decided to travel north back to the ocean, and then sort of loop around to the "part two" portion of our trip. We were still meandering:

The purposeful section of our journey—the search for my mom and dad—could wait a few days. We didn't know exactly what we were after, but we were certainly up for it. The Punta looked ready. Nothing had fallen off yet, as far as I could tell.

In an hour or two, we could see the ocean. The clouds momentarily parted. The radio sounded exactly like the radio we had left back home in America: the top forty. But no Kasey Kasem. Nevertheless, it sounded pretty good. We were driving along in Ireland with the windows down listening to that New Radicals song (the one where they keep saying, "You got the music in you"), and we were enjoying it. Ireland! A long-distance dedication for you, Eriu.

We cruised along the northern shore of Clew Bay. The beaches looked pretty good, so we stopped and decided to sample the waters.

Paulette is from Miami. She considers eighty degrees a good water temperature. I consider her a sissy with respect to water temperature. I grew up with the icy waters of the Jersey shore. I have been known to brave water that dipped into the frigid sixties. I'm a workin'-class cool-rockin' daddy.

We parked the car and headed out for our Celtic Surfin' Safari.

We had bathing suits with us, but we both considered it premature to change into them. First we would "test the waters."

The Irish beach wasn't much like the Jersey shore. There was no boardwalk, no cheese fries, and there were no "I'm With Stupid" T-shirts. There was no smell of frying dough. There were no cheese steaks. Still, it was a beach. When you walked on it, there was the satisfying feeling of the sand between your toes. It was July. Far off in the distance I thought I could hear Sinatra's "Summer Wind" wafting gently through the air.

July and we're at the other end of the ocean. This is what my parents were looking at many years ago.

I looked off to the distant horizon. Somewhere out there people were eating cheese steaks and riding the tilt-a-whirl. Somewhere out there was Bruce Springsteen.

I reached the water and took a tentative step.

My God.

I looked at Paulette.

It looked as if she was thinking, "My God."

We took a step back, but a tiny wave came in and covered our calves with water as cold as the gin in Sinatra's martini. Another wave came in and we were knee-deep in absolutely numbingly cold water. For a second, I wanted to show Paulette that I was an extremely tough-minded man who is not easily affected by outside stimuli. Then I went "Ahh!" in a high-pitched voice and threw my hands up and ran away from the water.

I was happy to see that Paulette did something similar. Wusses love company.

We ran back with quick short steps and lapsed into self-comforting arms-around-our-own-backs poses and stood there hopping quickly up and down. Paulette was jumping up and down, I believe, more than I was. Good, I thought.

"Shit! This is cold!" I said, unnecessarily.

"No shit," she said.

We decided to walk along the beach. It was quite beautiful and, after a mile or two, feeling returned to our calves, ankles, and feet.

We drove along, with the "Authentic Irish" station on. We stopped for a light lunch and my mind returned, as it must in Ireland at mealtime, to the potato.

The joke is, of course, "What's the thinnest book in the world?" The answer is, "Irish Cooking." "Italian War Heroes." "Great British Heavyweight Boxers" (until recently, anyway).

This is not really fair. We ate a wide variety of things in Ireland, and most were very good. Ireland isn't the South of France, but it's not the home of boiled meat either.

In Dublin there are a dozen world-class restaurants, but there are a surprising number of excellent places all over the Irish countryside. We ate great prawns outside Limerick and some fine lamb in Milltown Malbay. We had turbot in Mayo and memorable poached turkey near Newcastle. And, of course, multiple Irish breakfasts almost everywhere.

There is one item, however, that is on every Irish menu. Potatoes are served regularly with breakfast, lunch, and dinner. We saw boxty (grilled, pancakelike potatoes), champ (mashed with scallions), potato broth (peelings in sauce), potato and celery root puree (I can live without this one), Wicklow Pancakes (onions, potatoes, eggs, seared in olive oil), and Michaelmas salad (beets, scallions, dill, chopped eggs, boiled potatoes).

Paulette ate a lot of these (she passed on celery root puree). I watched her.

I have always hated potatoes. I have not eaten a potato in at least twenty years. The mere sight of a plate of mashed potatoes is often enough to ruin my day. Watching someone else eat mashed potatoes produces, in me, a deep feeling of revulsion. If I watch a television show on which people are eating potatoes, it makes me a little ill, even though I am not in the presence of actual potatoes.

I am a walking illustration of the efficacy of B. F. Skinner's ideas. Bernard Gannon and Anne Forde conditioned me to hate potatoes. My parents, being from Ireland, were pretty much addicted to potatoes. We would have mashed potatoes at every dinner. We would also have them for lunch. We would also have hash brown potatoes for breakfast. For a snack, there were always potatoes. My mom and dad would munch on a slice of potato while watching television or reading. Sometimes, when we went over someone else's house for a meal, my parents would look at the table with profound disappointment if the table happened to be lacking the magic ingredient. They would eat, but they would not be happy. In the car on the way home they would mention the lack of potatoes.

My mom: That was nice.

My dad: But why didn't they have potatoes?

When I had my own place I had dinner with my mom and dad. My dad looked around the table.

"What are you doing for potatoes?" he asked.

I thought, *Nothing! Potatoes aren't doing anything for me!* But I chickened out.

So, when I got the chance, I cut off the potato flow. No more potatoes. Never. Ever.

Once in a while people would ask me about it. I didn't know what to say, so I developed a stock response, a standard reply: In the late sixties, I remember seeing Johnny Cash say that he was going to wear black clothing until we got out of Vietnam. That sounded good to me. So, for a while, I said, "I am not going to eat potatoes until we get out of this senseless 'police action' in Vietnam."

We left, but Cash kept wearing black. I kept not eating potatoes. Then, when I read a little about Irish history, I thought I knew what to say.

"I will eat no potatoes because of the major tragedy that England caused involving Ireland in the nineteenth century," or something like that.

Then, when I got a little older, and read a little more about the horror of the famine, I felt really stupid that I ever said that. How could I trivialize something like that? So I stopped saying that.

But I still don't eat potatoes. I just don't like them and, at least in this lifetime, I never will. Potatoes in general are a pretty trivial subject. You've never seen "Potatoes" as a category on *Jeopardy*. You don't see many divorce cases where potatoes were involved. But in Ireland "potato" is a loaded word. "Potato" is to Irish people something like what "watermelon" is to black people. The mere mention of the word "potato" evokes in the Irish mind a complex hierarchy of emotions. At their simplest, "potatoes" are a meal. But the word "potato" also evokes something truly horrible and frightening, and it's something that will never go completely away from the Irish consciousness.

If you spend any time in Ireland you will inevitably hear about England's cruelty during the potato famine: That is a given. It doesn't matter if you stay in Dublin or roam around the countryside: Stay in Ireland for a few days and someone will mention it in your presence. Since the potato famine was 155 years ago, you would think it would become a seldom-mentioned subject, something for history class, something like (except for the PBS Ken Burns week) the American Civil War. If my stay there is typical, this is emphatically not the case in Ireland. In Ireland, the potato famine might have happened last year. Outside the universities, it's not usually discussed in any depth, but it's mentioned a lot.

I didn't keep any stats on it, but I literally could not get through a whole day in Ireland without having someone allude, in some fashion, to the famine. The first person I met when I got to Ireland, an old woman, had the following conversation with me while we waited for our luggage at the airport.

Woman: Are you visiting?

Me: Yes, from America.

Woman: First time?

Me: Yes, first time. My parents were Irish. They left when they were young and went to America.

Woman: A lot of Irish people had to leave. The famine.

Me: Yes, they told me about it. They left a long time after that, though.

Woman: Did they tell you about how cruel the English were? During the famine?

Me: Yes, they did.

Woman: They were awfully cruel.

Me: Yes.

*   *   *

It seems that Irish people aren't interested in talking in depth about the potato famine, especially to a Yank, but they do want you to "bear it in mind" while you are in Ireland.

The famine changed everything about Ireland, and the changes are still here today. Before the famine people in Ireland married young. After the famine they married late. Some said that the famine underlined the need for birth control, and Catholic Ireland took the only "nonsinful" course it had available and delayed marrying. It's more accurate to say that the famine was so devastating, people were not eager to share the horror of this world with children.

Before the famine, Irish was widely spoken all over Ireland. After the famine, English became the dominant language it continues to be in Ireland. The reasons for this are complex. They are dealt with in the definitive work on the potato famine, *The Great Hunger*. The book talks about what happened in a very thoughtful, controlled manner, but it is impossible to read the book without a deep sense of horror. It is, in its way, as disturbing as the Holocaust, or Stalin's mass murders in Russia.

A large part of that horror is the chilling realization that the whole thing wasn't an unavoidable natural disaster. If everything in Ireland's economy and food source weren't linked to the fate of that particular tuber, and England hadn't acted the way it acted, the potato famine might just be a footnote in the agricultural records of the era.

The agricultural reasons are simple enough. The famine was caused by the failure, in three seasons out of four, of the crop that basically fed most of Ireland, the potato crop. A fungal disease, *Phytophthora infestans,* often called potato blight, was the cause. No one knows for certain how the blight happened, but a lot of historians think that some fertilizer imported from South America might have caused it.

In another country, it wouldn't have been that bad. But in a country where the potato was, for many people, the basis

of the diet, it was an unimaginable disaster. Many Irish people of the era literally ate *nothing* but potatoes from cradle to
grave. The famine completely eliminated everything there
was to eat. Mass starvation was the result.

The blight actually began in Belgium, but Ireland was the
place where it had catastrophic effects. It began in the fall of
1845. Ireland was at the time a particularly big problem for
England. Seven centuries ago it had "conquered" its neighbor to the west. But it wasn't *really* conquered—"hearts and
minds"—and the newspapers of the era reflect that. But England certainly wasn't looking for another Cromwell-style
crushing. It was just collectively sick and tired of the ages-old
"Irish Problem." By 1845 England would have liked to just
forget about Ireland and its problems. It certainly tried.

In the early days of the famine, things really didn't go that
badly. The governments of Ireland and England set up soup
kitchens, but the scope of the problem was not immediately
evident. In England, the general feeling was that the "invisible hand" of the marketplace was not something that should
be tampered with. Economic nature should be allowed to
take its course.

A lot of the writings of the era reminded me of certain op-
ed pieces from the Reagan years in America. The government
doesn't need to get involved in an economic matter. The
markets have a way of regulating themselves, and so forth.
This has always been a convenient way of avoiding the problem of poverty. It probably always will be.

Ireland wasn't that easy to forget in those days but the English tried. They mostly attempted to publicly rationalize
what they were doing. Charles Dickens's Ebenezer Scrooge
was expressing a widely held English opinion when he suggested that conditions should be left to run free and therefore "decrease the surplus population." Malthusian solutions
were not considered completely out of the question

It is startling to come across the fact that since 1845, the
world's population has increased many times, while Ireland's

population has fallen by half. In the 1800s Ireland was the most densely populated nation in Europe. In 1845 a produce boat from America arrived, and everything changed.

In Ireland, the famine also revealed the unfortunate consequences of the traditional Irish religious faith. This line of reasoning went: All things happen because of God's great master plan. So "His will be done," even if it means a lot of children starve slowly to death. You can find this awful idea almost applauded in some of the Irish newspapers of the era. In England, of course, some ministers saw the blight as God's rightful punishment for the ungodly papists on their isle of the damned.

As the famine wore on, conditions produced more and more horrors for the rural Irish. The population had gotten used to a lot of potato-supplied Vitamin C. Scurvy reached epidemic status. As starving people crowded into food kitchens and public shelters, typhus became a huge problem. Typhus in its later stages produces delirium, and many of the infected Irish died truly horrifying deaths. "Many died screaming," reads a period report.

Nobody knows how many did die. The best estimates are over a million. In a country as small as Ireland in 1845, the famine was one of the great disasters of the modern world. One-fifth of the country died between 1845 and 1851.

The part of this that has really burned its way into the Irish mind is, however, not the magnitude of the deaths, however staggering. The part indelibly stamped on the Irish psyche is the utter ruthlessness of the landlords, as they evicted thousands and thousands of diseased and dying people who were not able to pay the rent on property for the land their families once "owned." And, of course, during the height of the famine, the final unthinkable horror, England exported grain from "food rich" Ireland. This fact, more than anything else, tortures the Irish psyche: "Let's get that train car of oats out of here; don't mind the dying people."

Many English landlords lived comfortable lives back in England, supported by the income-generating produce raised in Ireland. A lot of English landowners actually saw the famine as a good opportunity to evict their Irish tenants, tear down their little homes, and use the land for larger, more efficient farms. In the year 1850, an estimated 104,000 tenants were evicted.

Today there are revisionist historians who seek to point out that England could not really have done much more than it did. They try to explain the famine as an inevitability caused by a rapidly growing population and a rapidly failing economy. In Ireland, these arguments are not welcomed. The image of starving people being evicted from their own little homes and forced to live, without food, outdoors in an Irish winter is not something that easily fades from the mind. There were mass graves all over Ireland.

English government proclamations of the era are hideously cruel. A man named Charles Edward Trevelyan was put in charge of "Irish Famine Relief." He had this to say, ex officio: "Ireland must be left to the operation of natural causes."

Trevelyan also expressed his concern for the treacherous starving Irish: "If the Irish once find out there are any circumstances in which they can get free government grants, we shall have a system of mendicancy such as the world never knew." The sly Irishman will stoop to dying to get a free lunch, according to the justly despised Trevelyan.

The idea that this was all Ireland's fault was a popular one among the English. It appealed to their natural prejudice against the Irish, and it took England off the hook, morally speaking. The only way out for the Irish was to leave their beloved country. Staying at home meant certain death, but leaving wasn't much better. The Irish were packed into "coffin ships" bound for America. With little food and rampant disease, a great number died en route and were buried at sea. At least a million people died this way.

Many people say that it is pointless to blame England. After all, American ships brought the plague, and England did try to help. Still, for the Irish, particularly the Irish kid just discovering this in history class, there are too many mental images: English landlords evicting dying people; guarded train cars filled with food, winding through a land of starving women and children dying in slow, horrifying ways, reusable coffins with sliding bottoms opening to dump dead bodies; mass graves and coffin ships and drawings of a dying baby on a dead mother's lap. Too much.

When you look at Irish history, you have to wonder how the Irish-English hostility has lasted so long and is, even today, a given. After all, England treated Scotland and Wales pretty badly, yet, over time, those ancient wounds seemed almost healed. Why did England pick out Ireland for such singularly unspeakable treatment?

It may come down to one word: religion. Ireland is alone among northern European countries in its fervent Catholicism. The Reformation might as well never have happened as far as Ireland is concerned.

Because Ireland was, since Patrick, always decidedly pro-Catholic, the country has been on the "wrong side" in virtually every English brouhaha throughout modern history. Ireland was in the stands rooting for the Catholic Spanish Armada in 1588 when the English navy wiped it out. (In England, rowdies still yell "1588" at soccer matches.) Ireland was behind Napoleon at the beginning of the nineteenth century. It's hard to picture Ireland getting behind the eccentric French leader, but to a country in which religion is as important as it has always been in Ireland, that's the way it was. The Catholic side was always the Irish side, no matter who, or how horrible, the Catholic.

So every "God-save-the-queen" moment for England was a big defeat for Ireland. All of the big heroes in English history—especially Queen Elizabeth—are in the Irish Hall of Evil.

And the absolute bottom of the bottomless pit of Irish

misery happened in the 1840s, and it wrote its ugly story on the world's conscience. And the world blamed England. Travelers from Germany and France who happened to visit Ireland during this era strained themselves trying to describe the depths of human suffering they found there. The German J. G. Kohl, a veteran of observing misery, wrote that no form of life could seem pitiful after witnessing Ireland in the 1840s. All the misery he had seen before did not prepare him for the nightmare that rural Ireland had become in the 1840s. The worst suffering the well-traveled Kohl had ever witnessed was in Ireland. Kohl wrote: "Now I have seen Ireland, it seems to me that the poorest among the Letts, the Esthonians and the Finlander, lead a life of comparative comfort."

Frederick Douglass, of all people, was also a memorable witness to the potato famine. Douglass came to Ireland seeking a safe place. He had recently published his autobiography and, since he had mentioned his "owners" in the book, he no longer felt safe in America. Legally speaking, Douglass was a runaway. During the years of the potato famine, he could be legally "recaptured." He came to Ireland seeking asylum.

The choice of Ireland was, on the surface, odd. In the American South, a lot of the slave owners had Irish ancestors, and Douglass had actually written about the way Irish people had oppressed his people in America. Irish immigrants in America had organized African-Americans to control jobs in coal mines, railways, and shipyards. But he had also written that the Irish workers had encouraged him to escape from his life as a slave.

When Douglass first landed in famine Ireland, he was hesitant to draw any conclusions. Soon, however, after weeks of travel through the West of Ireland, he recognized that Ireland had a "terrible indictment to bring against England."

This whole Irish-English thing will probably never really end. Too much cruelty. Too much suffering. Nevertheless, in

1997, an amazing thing happened: England said it was sorry. Tony Blair officially "apologized."

"Sorry, chaps," he might have said, "bad show, that."

Around the same time, Emperor Akihito "apologized" for Japanese atrocities in World War II, and President Clinton "apologized" to African-Americans for that faux pas called slavery.

I'm sure everybody feels better now.

TEN

~ Catholics at Large ~

If you cruise along Ireland's northwestern shore, you have to fight the impulse to stop and take pictures. It is just beautiful. You circle Donegal Bay and stop at the little towns with strange names like Ballyshannon and Killybegs and you are having a grand time.

All is well in your Irish world as you drive along in your little wind-up car. You listen to a "real" Irish station that plays authentic Celtic music played on authentic Celtic instruments by authentic Celts.

We started to feel authentic. I was wearing one of those funny hats that authentic Irish people wear. I had worn it for days and it no longer even made me feel like an idiot. Or "eee-jit," to say it the way authentic Irish people like me say it. I had a sweater on that was quite Celtic in general appearance. Its label said L.L. Bean, but nobody had to know that. I looked at myself in the rear-view mirror. Yes, that's an Irishman there. You're lookin' at a fine broth of a man there.

I looked over at Paulette. I was now calling her Bridget. She was a fine broth of a Colleen. I think you might describe her complexion as "ruddy." She too was pretty tweedy. She was after looking pretty damn Irish even though her dad was born in France and her mom is from Saint Louis and her mom's mom was German. But Old Bridget, she was after being a fine slip of a lass. Old Bridget had a white sweater on and that's what her kind of Colleens wear.

On the radio they were havin' a "session" (that's what we call it). The bodhran was bodhraning and the fiddler was working overtime and you could almost hear them perspiring with the way they were playin' the reel. Everything was grand. It was brilliant.

I looked ahead and realized something that made me have a thought or two that was perhaps a bit *too* authentic. If we kept this up, if we kept driving where we were driving, we were going to be where things, I hear, are not that grand. We were going to be after driving into Northern Ireland. That was not in our nonplan. Before we left we stuck a note on the refrigerator: "No explosions."

I knew less about Northern Ireland than I knew about *southern* Ireland. All I know is what I saw on the television. What I saw on the television said, "No!" I'm sure that the northern part of Ireland is very interesting, but we knew that, for us on this trip at least, it wasn't going to happen.

We took the first right we could and headed for Monaghan. As we drove along, we decided that we were going to continue south by southwest. Drogheda sounded good. That was where Cromwell had done his damned work. But Cromwell was, at least, dead.

This didn't mean we were backing off on anything. We were still just rambling around Ireland. Still in phase one. Just free, we were. But we're not going to visit Northern Ireland. We're not getting *that* authentic, are we, Bridget?

No, we're not. Not this time. We'll go up there later.

As you cruise through northeastern Ireland, the part just south of "the troubles," you see a lot of really amazing churches—structures that dominate a lot of the little towns. These smaller Irish churches are quite beautiful. We tried to visit as many as we could. When we walked inside one, it seemed very natural to go over to a pew and kneel for a few minutes. This slowed us down, but then again, we weren't going anywhere in particular.

We visited the little churches at odd hours, but the

churches were always open, and there was always somebody in there. On our visit, I tried to read as many local newspapers as I could. I was always coming across editorials and features that told, in one way or another, of the decreasing influence of the Catholic Church in Ireland. Sometimes there were editorials that said that this was good. They said that now, with a little money and independence, the Irish person would no longer be a puppet of the Catholic Church. There were also editorials that said the opposite: that newly affluent Ireland was losing its spiritual center, the thing that made Ireland what it was.

Whatever the truth (and it's probably somewhere in between the two op-ed poles), the Catholic Church continues to have a greater influence on the population of Ireland than anywhere else in the world. Almost everybody in the southern, eastern, and western parts of Ireland is Catholic, and they seem much more aware of their status as Catholics than the average American Catholic. It has been this way for a very long time, since Saint Patrick arrived and turned the violent, pagan people into "the Land of Saints and Scholars who are, nevertheless, occasionally violent."

In many parts of Ireland, particularly in the west, Catholicism is a given. Nobody asks if you're Catholic. When we were in Mayo, I asked a close-to-if-not-already-drunk guy in his midtwenties about the local church schedule (it was Saturday) and he instantly rattled all of the mass times. I think if I had asked him what his name was, he would have given it quite a bit of thought, but he hit me with the mass times as if they were multiplication tables.

Ninety-two percent Catholic is the usual figure assigned to Ireland (excluding, of course, Northern Ireland, a separate country). Where I live now, the mountains of northern Georgia, things are quite a bit different. The Catholic population is perhaps 4 or 5 percent. Although a lot of the people have Irish-sounding names, Catholic churches are few and far between. Our priest, a wonderful man named Father Luis

Zarama, has to drive twenty miles on Sunday to say another mass up the road. Home-grown Catholics are very scarce here (Father Zarama is from Columbia).

Where I live, there aren't posted mass times. There's one service at nine and that's it. Miss that one and you're out of luck. Most places that we visited in Ireland have continuous masses at staggered times. Even in small towns, the churches were crowded every Sunday. The Irish masses I attended were much shorter than the Georgian variety. An Irish mass lasted, on the average, about twenty-five minutes, which is less than half the time a mass takes in Georgia.

You might think that the twenty-five-minute mass loses a lot of the reverence we associate with the service, but it isn't so. The services we went to were very beautiful and spiritual, with no sense of hurry. Just a "no pauses" policy. A Harold Pinter play done in the Irish Catholic manner would take about eighty-five seconds.

When I was in Ireland, and I happened to visit with someone, I would sit in the living room, look at the holy water fonts by the door, the Christ statue on the mantel, the crucifix over the table, the various religious pictures on the wall, and be brought back to my youth. I found it very comforting somehow, as if I were home again.

I was an altar boy, and so was my brother Bud, and we had priests and nuns who visited our house all the time. When I was little, the three visiting nuns were as much a part of Christmas as the Lionel train set. There was no mistaking us for Buddhists or Hindus or Protestants. During my childhood, we said the rosary every night.

When I was little, I really hated saying the rosary. Taking twenty minutes out of my life seemed awful. I never said so, of course, but my young brain found the whole experience—the kneeling and the recitation of prayer after prayer after prayer—almost unbearably boring. There was always the possibility, however, that my parents might forget to say the rosary. It had happened before. It was rare, but not impossible.

So every night, I would look at the clock as the evening, which had not yet included a rosary, rolled along. Eight o'clock would come. I would hope against hope that the unthinkable would happen, and my mother and my father would both forget about the rosary for an evening. It's not impossible, I would tell myself. Willie Mays dropped one fly ball. It can happen.

But my mother was an elephant about the rosary. It was *extremely* rare for her to forget. Her omissions were so rare that they burned themselves into my memory.

But my count, she made two. One time my dad got into a car accident. Another time Mom had the flu really bad (a normal virus would never cause a cancellation). A rosaryless evening in my house was an extremely rare event, but the watching of the clock made for great suspense.

It might get to be 9:15 P.M. I began to have some small hope that this time, she might, indeed, forget. There were no overt visible reminders. My mother didn't have a note on the refrigerator, but it was impossible to walk into our living room without thinking "Catholic."

My mom would get that look. She'd get up and say one word, "rosary," and another hope was destroyed. But, like a poor self-deluding slob with a lottery ticket, I always thought that I had a chance. Some nights the hands of the cuckoo clock in our living room would creep up toward nine-thirty and I would start to get anxious. Maybe they have forgotten. Maybe, this one night I won't have to kneel there and say the rosary. Sometimes I would start to sneak upstairs, get halfway up, and hear my mom say, "Hey, wait a minute. We have to say the rosary." And I would have to walk down, get the beads, kneel, and start praying.

When I think about those days now, I think that there are much worse ways of spending twenty minutes, but not back then. It seemed like forever. Twenty minutes is a long sentence when *The Twilight Zone* has a good episode. I remember many evenings of finishing the rosary and running over and turning on the television to hear:

John Roberts. A very ordinary man who took a very ordinary drive on a very ordinary evening and wound up not at the grocery store but in a place we call . . . the Twilight Zone.

It can't be the beginning. There are only two times Rod Serling talks: the beginning and . . . the end! I would close my eyes tightly and say bad words to myself. Another episode missed. I would think *I hate the rosary.* Then I would think about what I thought and think *I didn't mean that, God. Sorry! The rosary is fine. I enjoy it every evening. It's one of the highlights of my evening! Really. Sorry. What was I thinking! I didn't mean that "hate" comment.*

A rosary, for the non-Catholic, is a group of prayers that Catholics say that consists of a few Our Fathers and quite a few Hail Marys. You use the beads to keep track of where you are. (This was before Madonna made the rosary beads into a fashion accessory.) It's said out loud, so there's no faking it; you have to say every word. It takes about twenty minutes for a sincere person to say a rosary. For the fast talker it can take much less. (It would take about three minutes for certain people I've met in Los Angeles.)

The longest rosary I ever had was almost an hour. There was a visiting priest with us that night. I forget his name, but he had an amazingly deliberate manner. His Hail Marys were always punctuated with coughs and hems and haws. Sometimes he would pause in the middle of Our Father, take out a handkerchief, dab the corners of his mouth, excuse himself, and continue. For a little kid, dying to see *some* of *The Twilight Zone,* he was excruciating.

As he said his part of the rosary, a little familiar voice spoke to my brain:

Francis Xavier Gannon. A particular ordinary boy in a particularly ordinary house. A boy who knelt to say the rosary, but a boy who found, in a quite extraordinary manner, that he had missed . . . The Twilight Zone.

The rosary got to be a permanent part of my thinking—not the prayers; just the fact that I had to say it every night. I remember the first night I spent out of the house, sleeping over at a friend's house. I thought, around nine o'clock that night: *Damn, I don't have to say the rosary! Thank you, God. I'll never forget you for this!*

Then, after I thought about it for a while, I would add: *Not that I find anything wrong with the rosary, God. I wouldn't want you to get that impression.*

Once a week we would have all of the other Catholics on our street over for a big group rosary. I dreaded this: Company made the rosary last even longer. It was odd to hear those familiar words spoken by so many different voices. I thought that Mister Mich, who lived across the street, sounded like Fred Capasella, the Florida racetrack announcer I had heard hundreds of times owing to my dad's fondness for the track. Capasella's voice was a frequent background for dinner at our house.

When it was Mister Mich's turn to pray the rosary, I remember thinking of the various phrases as horses racing around an imaginary track in my mind. It's our father out in front. Who art in heaven on the outside. Followed by Hallowed be Thy name. Thy kingdom come on the outside . . .

The mind does strange things to you when you are ten years old and you listen to five million Our Fathers and Hail Marys and you know you have five million more to listen to. The racetrack rosary was only one mental game I played to pass the time. I imagined the beads were points that Wilt Chamberlain scored. I imagined they were home runs Mickey Mantle hit.

Nothing made the twenty minutes go faster.

My friends never had anything like the rosary ritual in their houses, even though a lot of them were Catholics. I felt a little uncomfortable talking about the nightly rosary ritual at my house, so I rarely mentioned it. I didn't want to seem like I belonged to a family of religious fanatics or something.

I didn't, of course. I belonged to a family of Irish people. When I had to interrupt, say, a wiffle ball game, and run home for the rosary, I would always say something like, "We're going out to get a frozen custard!" I don't think anybody really believed me, but it was a cover, so I used it.

But in Ireland, everything was different. At several B&Bs, I heard a familiar drone from downstairs: people saying the rosary. I didn't run downstairs and join them. *The Twilight Zone* is long gone, but I, a stranger, would be intruding. (That's what I told myself, anyway.)

Because I have a "Catholic Background," I found that I had something in common with everyone I met in Ireland. I found that I had an instant cache of conversational material. I would share rosary lore with them, chat about novenas I had made, quiz ex-altar boys on responses in the Latin mass. Check them out on the correct Catechism answers, that sort of thing. I felt like my dad talking to his buddies from World War II. Eccum spirie two-two-oh. God's phone number. Heh heh.

I also found it comforting to be around so many people who had some of the same religion-induced psychoses that I did. Just kidding, God.

In Ireland, *everybody* does the things that people thought were so weird about my family. Almost *every* house out in the west has holy water fonts next to the door. Almost *every* house has an Infant of Prague (a statue of the Christ child whose garb you change to fit the liturgical season). I didn't keep statistics but, on average, the houses I visited in Ireland had about eight crosses in them. There were signs with prayers and pictures of Jesus and Mary all over the place. I was in ten houses that had that famous picture of the sacred heart of Jesus. In Ireland I knew what it was like to be typical. Just another kid in a regular family. Everybody was looking around for the holy water font when they came into a room. Completely normal behavior.

In Ireland, I tried to walk inside every Catholic church I came across. There were, as you would figure, a lot of Saint Patrick's, but I also came across Saint Teresa's, Saint Peter's, Saint Joseph's, and the saint I'm named after, Saint Francis Xavier's. If you come across somebody named Francis in Ireland, you don't need to ask what his middle name is.

It was great to be in a country where my family was normal.

ELEVEN

~ Alcohol and the Irish Person ~

Phase one of our journey was near completion. We had only a few days of random rambling before phase two set in. In phase two we would no longer be footloose and fancy-free. We would be bound by an "agenda." We would have to look into very specific things, and we would probably be confined to very particular areas.

Our "plans" for phase two didn't look like plans. They looked like the two-pronged plan that had gotten me through much of my life until now, namely: 1) Make it up as you go along; 2) When convenient, pretend that you had whatever happened planned all the time.

So we drove along just north of Dublin without a mood of desperation. We had spent a lot more money that we thought we would spend, but when your money has James Joyce's picture on it, it's difficult to get upset. It's like Monopoly money.

But on that day in our lovely Punta, we decided to take stock. We would find a little town, find a pub, which is never hard to do in Ireland (like finding that name "Trump" in New York), and have a "sit-down." We wound up in a little pub around Dundalk, a town just north of Dublin on Ireland's east side. We found a seat, and decided to take stock.

Phase two, the finding of my parents, was still in front of us. It was time to get organized. We didn't want to leave without doing what we set out to do. Now that we had to actually act, our attitude changed. We were in a country that was still pretty foreign to us, and we had very little information. But Paulette was optimistic and I felt "if she is optimistic I am optimistic too." I had faith in Paulette and her orderly mind. When anybody loses anything around our house, she finds it. She always knows the ending of murder mysteries before everybody else does. She loves organizing. She loves lists of "things to do." She will have a "list of things to do" at my funeral.

We wrote a little list and evaluated it while we ate a few sausages and sipped another Guinness. (By then I could just walk in, sit down, hold up two fingers, and point. They always knew.)

There wasn't much on our list.

- Find out about Frank's dad
- Find out about Frank's mom.

At this point, we had a few regrets. We hadn't seen the whole country, but we had seen a good bit of it. Ireland is not the USSR. I'm sure we hadn't really seen and experienced Ireland, but we got semiclose. We had given it a good shot. We certainly used a lot of petrol. We had seen enough of it to get a pretty good impression.

But we knew that if we were going to accomplish our goals, we would have to draw a line someplace. We knew that, despite the vast uncharted Ireland that still lay before us, there were limits. We couldn't stay here forever, although that seemed, late at night, a very good idea many times.

We realized that we hadn't even set foot in Dublin, the city a lot of people think of when they think of Ireland. Dublin was the city of *Ulysses,* the city of Roddy Doyle's hilarious novels like *The Commitments* and *The Snapper,* the city of the Easter rebellion and certainly *the* city of Ireland.

I had even thought of going to graduate school there. Somewhere in the recesses of my brain I thought that I was an "Irish writer," even though I'd never spent a day in Ireland. I would go to Ireland and come home with my Irish degree and all would be well. I'd be a young man reconnected to his "Irishness."

It never happened, of course. When I was twenty-one, I already had a wife and a child (and twelve dollars on my nightstand, my "nest egg") and could never really afford to go to Ireland and study there. I remember sitting on a couch in Watkinsville, Georgia, and realizing that no matter what I did, I could never afford to go to Ireland and study.

But Yeats infected me. I said his poems to myself all the time. I thought they were perfect ways to spend the fifteen-minute tour around the factory that was part of the job.

I remember vividly opening the big gate in the back so they could unload the train at 7:30 in the evening. It was the only "thing" I had to do on my shift. The rest of the time was spent reading: Otherwise, I just walked around for insurance purposes "paying attention." Yeats was amazing. He would make the whole thing somehow elevated.

When I stood on the roof of the factory and turned the lights on, I thought about those swans. I made $1.75 an hour—pretty good.

A quarter after seven the sun would start to go down, and I'd open the King Kong–like gate; the train would gasp and belch its way in. They would unload the massive coils of wire. Forklift drivers would steer their amazing way over to it with startling quick turns of the little black steering wheel. The train would leave. I would close the door. All the time I would be thinking:

> Like a long legged fly
> Above the swift stream
> His mind moves upon silence.

I had always loved that stuff. In graduate school I loved
Yeats, memorized his poems, said them silently as I walked
around my rounds at Anaconda Wire and Cable Company,
where I was a security guard. It was my little world there. But
as I finished school, and started yet more school, and had another child, and moved to an opulent trailer in Winterville,
Georgia, I still found no matter what idignity the trailer park
had in store for me, I still loved that stuff.

So with Dublin before us and a big stack of American-
earned James Joyces in our pockets, we could go after Beckett or Joyce or Yeats or Shaw or Wilde (or the young,
still-living Heaney), or (for the politically minded) the chilling details of the 1921 revolution, but we thought that those
were very big fish and we weren't, after all, Ahab and his
wife. (Although Paulette, at times, reminded me of her.)

We wanted a *theme*, something that you could approach in
a more general way—something you could go after without
a lab coat, but some great generality that floated around Ireland, Literary Ireland, if it could be arranged.

We decided on our subject pretty quickly considering the
vast panorama of Ireland that presented itself to us. It was a
subject quite vast, yet a subject almost every Irishman had an
opinion about.

The Drink

My dad didn't drink very much and my mom didn't drink at
all. Even after thinking hard, I had to say that I never saw my
dad in the Irish state of "a drop taken." Even Saint Patrick's
Day and weddings never moved him to imbibe too much.

I have to admit that I don't really know many Irish people
who drink way too much. When I come to think about it, the
"problem" drinkers I know aren't even a little Irish. Nevertheless, on the official "Irish Day" (March 17) in America,
the standard thing to do is drink. You can also make jokes on

that day, but a great majority of them involve Irishmen and their fatal love for liquid refreshment. Of course, in America, people drink at Christmas. But they also open presents and do a lot of other things. On Saint Patrick's Day, there are no presents, just booze. Along with New Year's Eve, the focal point is alcohol.

In old American movies, whenever there is an overtly Irish man, he is often a guy who really likes to drink. He's often a funny, garrulous, likable guy, but he's also a drunk. In American movies "Irishness" is often almost exactly equivalent to the Irish character's fondness for booze. It might have nothing to do with reality, but in most American movies of the thirties, forties, and fifties, the connection is hard to miss. If the character you're playing is Irish you're going to be drunk and happy about it.

It's not just the movies that have linked alcohol and the Irish. If you wander down Broadway in New York City, it is difficult to walk a block without encountering a bar with an Irish name on the sign. There may be no real O'Brian who owns O'Brian's, but if you are stuck for the name of a bar, try one that starts with a "Mc" or an "O'." When they market a new alcohol product, they often name it after an Irish person.

In Ireland, *every* small town has a pub, and the pub owner has a well-defined, respectable role in the community. In the West of Ireland, everyone knows the pub owner, who is usually a very popular man.

So it wasn't surprising that my dad, an ambitious but poor Irish guy newly arrived in America, wanted to open a pub. He was, like so many of his post–World War II Irish-American brethren, doing what came naturally. "Gannon's Irish American Refreshment Parlor" was born.

There is, in Ireland, the pub-evaluation term, "good house." A "good house" is a place where a decent man might sit and have a glass or two without being bothered by things like fights and, as I heard it called in Ireland, "the general tumult of the world." In a good house a man can sit and sip his frothy beverages amid the company of other frothy beverage fans and be assured that he's not going to hear "It's All about the Benjamins" or something by Billy Idol. He's not going to encounter young men attempting to "converse with members of the opposite sex," unless those members are very, very familiar with those young men. Like they're married. No one is going to eat dinner, or fight, or attempt to make money, or, perish the thought, obtain illegal substances. No one is going to do anything that detracts from the main objective: drinking alcohol-laden beverages while sitting on tall stools.

Gannon's Irish American Refreshment Parlor, located in Camden, New Jersey, was a good house for twenty years. Then, in 1966, it became, for my dad, something else. Something less.

In October of that year a man walked into the liquor store area and asked for a six-pack of beer. The young man was overweight, bearded, and possessed a receding hairline. He was also seventeen years old.

The young man was on a mission. The American Beverage Control Board had sent him to Gannon's. The American Beverage Control Board was an organization charged with the unfortunate responsibility of determining whether every bar stayed within the law. The law in New Jersey at that time (it's since been changed) was that no one under the age of eighteen was legally allowed to buy alcoholic beverages. The inordinately old-looking kid was a shill for the American Beverage Control Board. Every year they hired some seventeen-year-old kid who looked to be much older than he really was. I don't know where they got these kids (the circus?). The kid "tested" bars by walking in and attempting to buy beer or liquor or wine. The kid would walk in, and if the bar sold him booze, he would leave and be followed in the door by the "ABC" men. Then the bar would be fined and shut down for a week. This was "fair" in Camden, New Jersey, and the gulag.

My dad hated paying the fine and he hated losing a week's

worth of business, but more than anything else he hated the fact that the ABC would run a notice in the local newspaper informing citizens that a bar had willfully broken the law. That really sickened him.

So Gannon's Irish American Refreshment Parlor was, in 1966, for a week at least, no longer a "good house." As the day for the announcement approached, my dad would grimly study the *Camden Courier Post*. His brow would wrinkle in concentration as he sat in the big green upholstered chair that was his and his alone. Dad's chair sat in the corner of our living room right next to the console RCA television with the statue of the Blessed Mother on top. Woe to he who sits in that chair if his name isn't Bernard Gannon.

When the day of the axe finally arrived, I was sitting on the living-room sofa. It was about six o'clock in the evening. My dad stared at the paper with a blank look. He jerked involuntarily when he got to the legal notice informing the public of his "crime." He read the notice, read it again, put down the paper, took off his glasses, stood up, and walked quietly upstairs. His face was the face of a man walking to the gallows. He stayed up there for the rest of the night. My mom went up to talk with him. I didn't go near him. I just sat on the sofa and watched him slowly walk up the steps. A crushed man.

He took it hard. He had always lived in dread of the ABC. He thought they were unfair, but his dread of them was almost frightening. Before his infraction, he talked of the ABC often. He rarely called them "the ABC." He called them "the cursed ABC," as if "cursed" was part of the organization's name. He pronounced it "ker-said." It emphasized, in an almost biblical way, his intense hatred for the vile organization.

He talked about the cursed ABC with such bitterness that I remember wondering as a child why my dad hated those alphabet letters that were always in the front of my classroom right under the picture of God at Saint Cecilia's Grammar School. (I confused easily as a child. Still do.) The cursed

ABC was worse than the boogieman. The cursed ABC will find you. The cursed ABC will find you and, when he finds you, *"He will ruin you for life!"*

Now, in 1966, just when I had left Saint Cecilia's Grammar School for Camden Catholic High School, the worst had happened. By then I thought of it as some vague horrible event in the future. Now it was here. The cursed ABC had found my father. The cursed ABC had found my father and ruined him for life.

The total devastation of my father was published in the *Camden Courier Post*, the local venue for devastation announcements. It was printed in tiny print and buried on a page near the back of the paper, but for my dad, it might as well have been tattooed on his forehead. For my father, it was Hester Prinne all over.

ALCOHOL CODE VIOLATIONS, CAMDEN: Gannon's Irish American Refreshment Parlor. Sale of alcoholic beverages to a minor.

He had to pay a fine and close the bar for a week. When he was asked why the bar was closed, he said that he was doing some renovation.

The bar reopened, of course, but things could never again be all right. Something very valuable had been taken from him. It was something that could never be returned.

He knew, deep in his Irish psyche, that Gannon's Irish American Refreshment Parlor, a place into which he had poured his soul, was no longer a "good house." The cursed ABC had finally gotten him.

My dad took the whole thing much more seriously than he should have. For a couple of years he stopped attending Saint Cecilia's Church. The church was a block from our house (church proximity was a major factor in my mom's choice of residence), but on Sundays my dad would get up even earlier than he normally did and drive fifteen miles to another Catholic church. In that distant church, he was anonymous; no one knew of the place and the cursed ABC.

I am sure that no one but my dad thought of the liquor bust, but no one could tell him that. He was like a Nathaniel Hawthorne character, a man haunted by his "sin." He would ask me every week if anyone had mentioned "the thing" (he could not give it any other name). I would always tell him "No," but he would stare deep into my eyes, searching for any sign of deception.

Over the next few years, "the thing" was a frequent subject of discussion among the family, but we were very careful never to mention it outside the house. But around the dinner table, or driving to work, I heard the story many times. Each time it gained details. The kid the ABC hired got older and older looking (he was eventually bald and bearded with a lot of gray in his beard). If my dad had lived longer, the ABC kid would have looked older than he did. Eventually, my dad hinted that he strongly suspected that the American Beverage Control Board frequently resorted to cosmetic surgery. Nothing was beyond them. They were controlled by Satan, and they did his work.

My dad's brother, Uncle John, told me that my dad had talked about owning a pub from the time they were little kids back there is West Meath. According to John, Bernie Gannon thought that pub ownership was a great calling, second only to the priesthood. When William Butler Yeats described an Irishman's ambition as "doing the most difficult thing that can be contemplated without despair," he was certainly talking about Bernard Gannon, the hopelessly poor kid who wanted to own his own pub.

Sometimes I would catch my dad just standing motionless outside Gannon's Irish American Refreshment Parlor. He would just stand there with a very serene look on his face: portrait of a man in love.

My dad's attitude toward his pub was very typical of first-generation Irish. If mythology says something very basic about the people who produced it, we can see an ancient love/hate relationship between the Irish and the drink. For the Irish, as has been often noted, mythology and history tend to be blended, and this is very evident in their ancient myths. These things didn't "happen," but in a very real sense, they are always happening.

The ancient Irish worshiped nature gods who lived in a world named Tir Nan Og, "the Land of Eternal Youth." The big book is called *Lebor Gabala Erenn,* the book of "the taking of Ireland." The book records the lives of six races of Irish inhabitants. Some are human, some divine, but, as in the Greek myths, everyone acts more like human beings than like gods.

The gods are creative beings (poets, artists), and the regular people are farmers. The regular people finally "win" Ireland, and the gods have to hide themselves in nature. They live in the beautiful parts of Ireland, which is almost everywhere.

These regular people are called the "Gael." Their enemies are the Fomor, a race of one-eyed giants who live in the ocean. The great hero of Ireland is Finn mac Cumhal (often called Finn mac Cool). He marries a woman named Murna, and they have a son Ossian. They lived long enough to interact with the fellow who was responsible for replacing all this with Christianity, Saint Patrick.

The Vikings destroyed the old writings about Finn mac Cumhal, so the oldest extant one dates from 1453. The book *The Boyish Exploits of Finn mac Cumhal* tells the story of Finn and Saint Patrick sitting down, having some drinks, and talking about things. In some versions, Saint Patrick actually turns old Finn into a Catholic. In some of them Finn remains a pagan. In the version where he rejects Catholicism, Finn's son Ossian tells Saint Patrick what the best things in life are: "To share bowls of barley, honey and wine." Even mythological Irishmen know, in the words of Flann O'Brian, "A pint of plain is your only man."

*   *   *

Because alcohol and Ireland are so linked in the public mind, there are, according to my research, 21,982 jokes involving Irish people and alcohol. (All right. I made that up.) The archetypal joke is the one that follows. This is the Irish/Alcohol joke that exists in Plato's world of essences. It's labeled "*The* Irish/Alcohol Joke."

An Irishman is standing outside a hospital with a look of great worry. He seems on the verge of tears and he implores passersby. A wealthy Englishman approaches.

Irishman: "Sir, please help me. My wife has to have an operation or she will die, and they won't do it unless I can raise one thousand dollars. Please help me."

Englishman (seeing how distraught the Irishman really is): "Here is your money. God bless you!"

Irishman: "And God bless you, sir!"

Englishman (as an afterthought): "And you look like you haven't slept in days. Here's a pound. Go have yourself a drink and calm down."

Irishman (refusing the money): "Hey, I have drinking money."

This is generally acknowledged to be the "Danny Boy" of Irish drinking stories.

The Irish fondness for alcohol, like many ugly racial stereotypes, turns out to have some actual, sociopsychological validity. It is, of course, impossible to get a full set of data on the subject. How do you measure "fondness" for alcohol? And, until the twentieth century, people didn't go around compiling statistics on everything. Nevertheless, concerning the Irish-American, the evidence seems to point a massive finger at the Celtic drinker.

In 1909, an early academic (with a very academic name), Maurice Parmalee, compiled some statistics on Irish-American drinking habits. He used, as his lab, the city of

Boston, a place crawling with Irish guinea pigs. As his barometer, Parmalee used the total number of various ethnic groups arrested for public drunkenness in Boston that year.

His results confirmed an ugly supposition. In the game of public drunkenness, the Irish were the big winners. Belgians, Scotsmen, and Canadians all scored above average, but the Irish took home the gold. (Unfortunately, this never became an Olympic event.) Other early studies showed the same result. Among "alcoholic case admissions" to a state hospital in 1900, the Irish were, once again, the clear winners. It wasn't even close. The percentages broke down this way: Irish 37 percent. The Germans, English, and Scotch vied for the silver with scores in the low 20s. The Jewish population had a microscopic 5 percent.

Richard Stivers, a professor of sociology at Illinois State University, has written the definitive study of the subject, *Hair of the Dog*. His well-argued thesis is that a negative stereotype was foisted upon Irish-Americans, but that later, Irish America actually used the stereotype to construct a mythical, positive image of the tippling Irishman. This "positive" image is the charming, funny, harmless drunk we see in so many American movies and plays.

So the myth is, well, a myth. Andrew Greeley, an academic and sociologist as well as a best-selling novelist (and an Irish-American), had this to say after going over what was, by the end of the century, a mountain of data: "Among drinkers, the Irish are no more likely to have a serious alcohol problem than are many other groups in United States society."

However, the Irish are unique in *celebrating* their drinking, in presenting it as an endearing aspect of their culture. They got together, noticed the problem, and had a party for it. "A toast to pathological drinking!"

Whatever else you can say about that, it is *so Irish*.

Everywhere we went in Ireland, the subject of alcohol seemed to bob to the surface at one point in the evening (often late). So it seemed pretty clear that the Irish/booze equation has not completely vanished from the Irish mind. Despite the fact that Dublin is the hub of the new "Celtic Tiger" economic boom in Ireland (can't see Gordon Gecko as a drunk), it is also the home of countless bars. It is very difficult to walk for five minutes in the town and not pass a drinking establishment. Nevertheless, it seemed to me, that by, say, 2050, the whole Irish/booze thing may be gone from the public mind. The big factor, I think, is all these dot-com kids walking around Dublin with the cell phones glued to their ears.

Half of Ireland is under twenty-eight years old, and almost a third of the population is either in college or already college-educated. Almost 60 percent of them have or are about to earn a degree in business, engineering, or science. Partly because of this, a whole lot of American companies have set up shop in Ireland in a major way, and a lot more are about to follow suit. IBM, Oracle, Motorola, Northern Telecom, Microsoft, Sun, and many, many others are solidly established in Ireland. They even have their own version of Silicon Valley (they call it the "Silicon Bog"). Ireland is a great place to do high tech. There is a young, well-educated workforce, a favorable tax situation, a booming economy, an inviting government, and many other protech factors. In the twenty-first century Ireland isn't going to be Yeats's "ancient dreaming race." There will be a lot more Gordon Geckos than Darby O'Gills.

In a way, this will be very sad. It makes me feel horrible to think of County Mayo turning into Westchester County. There is, however, for me, a bright spot: I'll be dead when it happens.

While we were in Dublin, we were glad to see that we weren't alone in bemoaning the inevitable. There were frequent editorials in the papers and on the television that had, as their general theme: "When Ireland gets rich, are we going to turn into the English?"

A frightening thought. We kept out minds off this by pursuing our academic study, tentatively titled, "What is it with Irish people and booze?" Throughout Dublin, I found a lot of people who wanted to talk about it. Of course, I always asked about it in pubs, so my study might have lacked scientific validity. Still, it was fun.

I heard a strange sentence more than once: "We have fun with the misery." In general there seems to be three opinions: A, Drinking is good; B, Drinking is bad; and C, Complete and utter ambiguity.

The clear winner seemed to be "C." Even the clichés were ambiguous. I saw these words framed in a pub: "Drink is the curse of the land. It makes you fight with your neighbor, it makes you shoot at your landlord, and it makes you miss."

Among those in category "A," the defenders of drink, the most popular defense is some version of, "Pubs are not for drinking; they are for conversation." Since every pub we walked into had a loud, continuous, neverending (or even pausing) collective conversation, there was something to this argument. But, as was pointed out to me by a member of the "B" party, "There are no Starbucks in Ireland."

An English major can't walk around Dublin without thinking of *Ulysses* and, in thinking about the book and Dublin, thinking about alcoholic beverages. As Bloom says in the novel, "A good puzzle would be (to) cross Dublin without passing a pub." Indeed, at the Guinness Brewery at Saint James Gate, there's a museum dedicated to the formal study of beverage-imbibing. Dublin is a lot more than the sum of its pubs, but the city seemed a great place to get clinical about the Irish and the drink.

Drinking beverages that contain alcohol leads to many things. In *Macbeth*, Shakespeare said that it led to three things: sinus problems, excessive urination, and lechery. He pointed out that the last symptom was helpful in the prologue to the event, but a hindrance in the performance of the same. Time has confirmed him as the wisest of Englishmen, an admittedly handicapped contest.

It also, of course, leads to violence and craziness and appearances on the television program *Cops* clad only in underwear. Fighting and booze are forever married in the Irish consciousness. John Wayne's epic fight with Victor McLagen in *The Quiet Man* was punctuated, quite appropriately, by a midbattle stop at the local pub. If you're Irish, goes this line of "thought" (hammered home in countless movies), you drink, and if you drink, you fight. It makes things rather simple.

Recently the field of magnetic imaging achieved the technological ability to determine the exact points at which a human brain processes certain stimuli. Research scientists can now actually "observe" an idea. There is an identifiable place in the brain that responds to abstract ideas like "cuteness" and "morality." The amygdala goes off when it sees little puppy dogs. A portion of the orbitofrontal cortex generates activity when asked about the death penalty.

The sections for "Irish" and "Crazy" are, in the collective American brain, the same place. It's difficult to say exactly when the "Irish" site appropriated the "Crazy" site, but the site for "Irish" contains "Crazy" as well as "Cop," "Love of Mother," and so forth. Billy Conn's explanation of why, far ahead on pints, he tried to knock out Joe Louis and got ko'ed himself: "What's the use of being Irish if you can't be crazy?" turns out to be a very prescient observation by the Pittsburgh Kid.

Irish America wants "Crazy" to be seen as "Lovably Deluded" rather than "Psychotically Anomalous." We want using, "Heck, he was just being Irish," as an excuse to carry some legal weight.

The fighting Irish. Good participle, and, in my limited experience, largely true. I know several Irish guys who are, in toto, a big pain in the ass. The kind of guy who will, when aroused, attack a towel machine. No less a man than Paddy

Flood, boxer trainer and ubermick, put it best: "The Irish love trouble like no other race. When God made the Irish, He made 99 percent of them Iagos."

I am Irish and I don't ordinarily love trouble. Yet, in a car wash in Demorest, Georgia, it found me. We had a brief relationship. I actually punched a guy in the mouth. It was on Sunday afternoon and no alcohol was involved. There was just something about that guy. Something that said, "Please punch me," to part of my lymph system. So I did.

I had just finished listening to "Born to Be Wild" on the radio. If I had been listening to Kenny G it might never have happened. I was driving a Volvo, the least aggressive car in the world. I pulled into the little car wash. I took out the two plastic mats and hung them up on those hook things. I started vacuuming out my pacifistic Volvo.

A guy in a pickup truck drove in. No one else was there. There were three stalls. Nevertheless, he selected the one labeled "trouble." He didn't know that he was in the company of Irish people. Me. I finished vacuuming and went over to ask him something. I left the vacuuming before my fifty cents worth of vacuum was over. I courteously wanted to get to him before he put his three quarters in the box to activate the "wash" experience. I was concerned and utterly affable. If you saw me you would say that I looked like the nicest guy in the world. Mr. Friendly.

"Excuse me," I said. My body language said that I was sorry that I had to inconvenience him in any way. "I have my mats hung up in that stall and the other two stalls don't have those hook things for mats, so could you move to another stall?"

"No," he said.

I could have said, "What?" or something. Or I could have just taken the mats down. My original reaction was "take down the mats and make a nasty sarcastic comment." That's the reaction that I was acting on when I looked at him. He had what I interpreted to be a smirk.

So I did what anyone would do, any card-carrying *Irishman*. I punched him in the mouth.

He didn't fall down and my hand started to *throb*. He sort of stumbled against his truck. But I did see that he was amazed and shocked at what the old guy with the Volvo had done. Then he said the words that made it all worthwhile.

"You're crazy," he said, and I thought, *I think I just broke my hand but I am happy*.

Later, of course, the unfortunate moral side of me made me feel really bad. At the same time, the physical side of me was leaning on the pain button.

But the Irish part of me said, *Nice going*.

The Experiment

I decided, like Doctor Jekyll, to use myself as a guinea pig in my investigation of the connection between booze and the Irish. I was Irish, so I was walking around with my own handy laboratory. Paulette is, regrettably, not Irish, so she was not a subject for study in this clinical situation. I decided that I would go to a pub in Ireland and drink until I became intoxicated. Then I would carefully record my data.

So we went to a pub at approximately 9:30 P.M. I then consumed several pints of Guinness, more than enough to achieve my clinical goal. Paulette was not quite a designated driver. She had also consumed a few. There was a live band playing Irish music. They got better and better as the evening progressed.

We met some young Irish people, Robbie and Lief. Lief was a girl. They had been dating for a few years. Lief told me that they like to go to pubs quite a bit. Robbie liked it a little more than she did. He seemed to want to do this on a regular basis.

As an elder, I counseled him. I told him that it wasn't a good idea to get wasted. As I told him this, we drank glass after glass of semipotent beverage until well after an hour when decent people were asleep. It was fun to travel to a distant country and then drink too much, even if it was a scientific experiment.

By around two, the place started emptying out. It was a Tuesday, and as Robbie told me, it was a good idea to stop drinking at 2:00 A.M. on a work night. We said our goodbyes in the near-empty pub. I was quietly proud that we had, indeed, "closed the place."

That was when a quiet horror gripped us.

Our Punta, our red, little, comforting Punta, was gone.

At first we controlled our panic by walking up and down the street. Paulette suggested that perhaps we should call either our B&B or, maybe, the police. Our Punta was gone.

I was, despite the nine Guinnesses, amazed and appalled. Criminal activity in a lovely land like Ireland! What a world we live in! If I hadn't been drunk I'd have been even more appalled. As we walked through the streets and slowly got used to the idea that yes, our car had been stolen, various near-desperate ideas ran through our alcohol-addled brains (okay: *my* alcohol-addled brain). Paulette offered the opinion that the group of Irish youths gathered near the corner might perhaps be a sort of *Clockwork Orange* ultraviolence group. I could not assure her that that was, indeed, not the fact. I reminded her that *Clockwork Orange* was set in *England*. It was also fictional, I think.

We wandered up and down the street, searching in vain for our vehicle. The truth still hadn't quite sunk in. Our rented car was gone. And it would remain that way. Our bright red minicar, the Punta, was now gone. Gone forever. Someone could write an opera about this.

I thought of what things we had in the car. Not much. This wasn't so bad. Tomorrow we'd call the rental place. It probably happens all the time. We walked a few desultory blocks, up and down. We had no car. I had no car *and* I was

drunk. We were walkers. We were losers. I was a drunken
loser.

We happened to see a woman, an attractive woman, actually, but with an alarmingly white face. She looked like a
woman in a Toulouse-Lautrec painting. But she didn't seem
to be a lady of the evening, even though she was standing in
the doorway of a shop.

Paulette called out to her, and the woman with the white
face responded to the desperation in Paulette's voice.

"Please," said Paulette, "I think our car has been towed.
Do they tow cars here?" I hadn't thought of that. I made a
mental note: *Drunkenness in an Irish person often leads to stupidity.*

"Yes, they tow cars here, but not often," said the white-
faced woman, who was beginning to remind me of the ladies
in *Cabaret*. "I am sure they did not tow your car. What kind
of car was it?"

"It was a rental," I said, "a little red something-or-other."
I could not bring myself to say, "Someone stole our Punta."

"Are you sure it was parked here?" asked Lotta Lenya.
"The block over looks exactly like this block."

"Oh, no," said Paulette. "I know that it was right here."

I remembered the name of the store we had parked in
front of. (I couldn't remember it now without a whole lot of
sodium pentothal.)

"You know," she said, "there is another store with that
name."

I told her that I was sure we were parked in front of *this*
store. At that moment I wasn't sure of anything, but I
faked it.

"Ah," said the woman with the white face. *What did that
"Ah" mean?* I thought.

Paulette and I looked at each other hopelessly. We were
now sure that our car had been stolen. Stolen in Ireland. We
came looking for our ancestors and someone stole our car.

I tried to be philosophical.

"Hey, we'll call the police," I said. "It will be an adventure."

At that point the white-faced woman said, "Is this your car?"

I looked at the car. It looked a little bit like our car. As a matter of fact, it looked just like our car. But it was gray. Our Punta was red.

But I looked at the car. It looked, except for the color, *exactly* like our car. I moved closer. I looked in the window, and what I saw was startling.

The car had my "Irish" hat on the backseat. Maybe it was somebody else's hat. They have those hats all over Ireland. Every Irishman owns one.

I looked at the woman. I realized (much later than a rational person should have realized) that her face was so white because many of the streetlights in Ireland are yellow. Take a little red car; stick it under one of those lights. It looks kind of gray. Oops.

Yes, it was our car. If I had drunk nine glasses of sodium pentothal, I still should have realized that.

"Well, that's good for you," said the white-faced woman. She gave us a little smile. I looked at my hands. They looked white. Golly. Science in action. Spectrum stuff or something. Why hadn't I paid attention in high school?

We got into the Punta and waved to the white-faced woman as we drove back to our hotel. Paulette, of course, drove. I felt pretty stupid. I also felt pretty drunk. But the evening wasn't a total loss. I had real clinical evidence of the effect of alcohol on the Irish brain.

TWELVE

～ *Dublin: End of Days* ～

Dublin is a great city, a city where you can find anything that you are seeking. It's the sort of place that you could spend a year in and still miss many, many things. We had two days. Rather than run around trying to squeeze in as much as possible, we continued with our casual meandering manner. It had been good to us so far, so why change now? We would miss a lot, but we knew by now that we would be returning more than once.

If the West of Ireland seems like the nineteenth century, Dublin is right on the cutting edge of 2002. The population is a million and a half, but I got the strange impression from talking to people in Dublin that everybody knows each other. Nobody calls Dublin a "city." It is a "town." As in the rural parts of Ireland, the people were unfailingly friendly, and it is much harder *not* to get into a conversation than it is to begin one. Dublin is by far the friendliest large city I ever experienced. I'm not much of a world traveler, but Dublin seems friendlier than any large American city. Other Americans we met told us the same thing. I have no theories about this.

Like New York, Dublin has the horribly poor and the abominably rich right next to each other. You can see serious-suit guys with their cell phones glued to their ears, and they're walking by buildings where you can make out wash-lines hung in the rear.

Dublin circa 2002 is the epitome of a "boom town."

Housing prices have gone up over 25 percent in the last year, and its economic growth rate stays about 8 percent. You can almost feel it grow as you walk around, but it grows, like New York or a teenage boy, vertically, not horizontally.

A lot of places in Dublin have the juxtaposition of the old and the new. There are bars that look as if H. G. Wells and E. M. Forster should be sitting at a corner table, but the second floor of the same building looks like *Clockwork Orange* with an Irish accent.

Many of the major streets in Dublin are the polar opposites of the roads in rural Ireland. They were the widest streets I've ever seen. I couldn't really tell you how many "lanes" of traffic there were. The moving cars are only rarely in a straight line.

It's a great city for strolling, but a better city for stopping completely. You can't walk twenty-five feet without seeing someone standing still or seated. Dublin is New York in the Bizarro world: I never saw anyone who was obviously in a hurry.

Even though it's a huge city, it seems to invite you to take it easy. The park, Phoenix Park, is huge. It seems appropriate that the largest area in the city is dedicated to nothing more serious than walking your dog. There are a lot of statues in Dublin. I saw a tour guide with some tourists and I thought he was talking about statues. He was pointing at them, anyway. I eavesdropped. He was talking about a statue of William of Orange that was exploded, melted down and rebuilt, and then exploded again. William of Orange was not unique. The tour guide talked about many other statues of famous people that the Irish had exploded.

Maeve Binchy has said that a good way to write a novel is to go Ireland, go into a pub, sit down, and listen. Dublin is probably the best place to do this in Ireland. Some people would argue with that and say that the west is conversation central in Ireland, but my vote goes to Dublin. The west is more charming, but in the "pub talk" category, I've got to go with Dublin. I vote for Dublin because of the *range* of talk you can get there. If you look hard enough you can find almost any kind of conversation you like. The conversational range is vast: from meandering tale to urban speed-talk. The way Irish people use English is always amazing, and compared to a lot of American talk, it's like listening to a guy come in and play something on the piano after you've listened to a guy tuning it for an hour. If the English language were an electric guitar, Dublin is Jimi Hendrix. Most of America plays on a Yanni album.

In Dublin pubs, the simplest sentences can become a tangled web of words. I spent a few years teaching high-school English and, for me, Irish talk was an amazing experience. No subject-verb-object. No present or past tense. Questions are answered by questions. Sometimes statements are questions. Everything has already happened, and we are recalling it or we're pretending we're in the future and we are describing it. Are you after having read that? Is it the next sentence you're after?

That may make it sound as if it's difficult to understand (for a Yank). It isn't at all. It does make you pay attention, though. After having spent some time in Dublin I no longer think that James Joyce was a completely and utterly unique writer. He was just really good at Irish.

I am, I think, the only member of the extended Gannon family who ever got paid for producing words, but I am, to be honest, not in the top ten as a word producer, and I haven't even met a lot of my extended family. I may be in the bottom of the top hundred, but by that statement, I'm being nice to myself. Irish people naturally love words. I am the only one in the family who ever wrote them, that's all. I wouldn't put a patch on an Irish writer's ass, as my mom would say.

My childhood was surrounded by words. A whole bunch of weddings and get-togethers and wakes and what-have-yous. I grew up in a big swirling ocean of words. They were technically "English," but in every way that matters they were Irish words, or at least "Irish-English." There was an occasional dip into Gaelic, but my mom and dad didn't want us to know that language. It's a cliché to say that Ireland has an "oral tradition," but it's more than a tradition. Silence must be filled. I remember many long, crowded car rides where a "Pinteresque pause" was, at the most, three seconds.

When I was little, very little, I was "the quiet one." My mom told me that they would sometimes forget me because I was so quiet. I was not quiet. I was just waiting for a break in the conversation.

My first memories are of this endless torrent of words. An unending spiel. Even when someone died, they would put the deceased out there in his coffin, then they would talk to him anyway. The next day, they'd take him out and bury him. Then they'd go back to the house and talk about him.

If they ever had a world competition for talk, Ireland would be a dominant nation. They would be like the Cuban boxing team or the Russian weight lifters. When I brought Paulette home to "meet the family" there was an awkward period. This lasted eight seconds.

In Ireland, no matter where we went, it was the same. We would walk into a pub, sit down, and in ten minutes, be into a deep conversation about something. It could be trivial or profound, but it was, invariably endless. Talking in Ireland is breathing. When you stop talking in Ireland, you are dead. Then they will no longer talk *to* you. They will talk *about* you. They will say many, many things about you. If you have led a truly exemplary life, "the life of a saint," only half of what they say will be bad.

You can't spend time in Dublin without thinking of writers. We wandered into the staggering library of Trinity College and looked at the long line of white marble busts in the great hall. You can't avoid the writers. Many of them would be shocked to see that they've made it to this room. When they were alive, Ireland sure wasn't thrilled with them.

A Dubliner who taught at Trinity told me that some writers earn a greater honor than a place in the Trinity University library. They have pubs named after them.

The Pubs of Dublin would be a massive tome. More likely, it would be a multivolume set. Dublin is like a drinker's heaven. The bars, as far as I can tell, haven't one single video game, and they all seem to have booths.

There are always a few old guys who are as serious about drinking as Elton John is about Lady Di. There are also several guys who look like they belong somewhere near Fifty-seventh and Park. These groups never interact.

The sheer number of Fifty-seventh-and-Park guys is startling, as dense as downtown Manhattan at five in the afternoon. If all the cell phones in Dublin went off at the same time it would destroy eardrums.

The whole Hermes tie-wearing set is also startlingly young in Dublin. Over half of the 1.5 million people look like they could be in the Irish version of *Friends.* A lot of these guys work for American companies. Microsoft Europe is in Dublin, and Dell and Hewlett-Packard also have their European bases there, but there are also monster home-grown computer firms: Iona and Trintech.

There are theories about why Ireland is so tech-friendly. I've read that the Celtic mind is naturally cyber-ready, but I'm a walking argument that the Irish brain, even after prolonged exposure to American technology, is still quite dinosaurlike in its resistance to high tech. But I am an old Irish guy. Among Dublin's population I would be considered a pronounced elder. Dublin's silicon group looks like the senior class at Cal Tech.

Like every other place in Ireland, Dublin has some amazing churches, and these are much larger than the usual town church. Among the most striking is St. Mary's, with its soaring steeple looking down over Parnell Square. Even though it's a church, it looks threatening. It's called "the Black Church." That's its color, but it also seems to describe its menacing aspect. If they wanted to make the movie *The Irish Omen,* that would be a good place for something scary and terrible to happen.

It would be, for a guy like me, a nightmare to drive in Dublin. I would be an even-money bet to get lost every ten minutes. Every street seems curved. We went for a two-hour walk. I strolled along thinking that Paulette was keeping track of where we were going. I finally asked her. She said she thought I was keeping track.

We asked several people and we received very friendly but utterly incomprehensible directions. I have a hard time with directions given in slow American English. In Irish English, I'd be better off reading the Rosetta Stone.

As we were wandering around half-lost reading street signs, I had a flash of recognition. I felt that somehow, I had seen these street names before. When you are lost in Dublin, and you went to college, you are inevitably thinking of that big black book that begins with that giant S . . . "Stately, plump, Buck Mulligan . . . " *Ulysses!* It was finally going to be of some use to me.

It is a good, but intimidating idea to read *Ulysses* before coming to Dublin. You can then walk along with the book's characters and visit the same places Joyce immortalized in the book. Joyce's book is set on June 16, 1904. That is also Paulette's birth date (month and day, not year). As I was an English major, that explains my fascination with her.

I read Joyce's book in college, and I remember it as being rare and among the only difficult-to-read books that were actually worth the trouble. It's hard going, but has some truly amazing and funny parts and is, in every sense, a real literary masterpiece.

Every June 16, Joyceans from around the world come to Dublin and live "Bloomsday." They dress like Joyce (an easy Halloween choice: eye patch, glasses, semi–Fu Manchu) or one of the characters in the novel and, if they follow the book closely, end the day drunk. As you walk around Dublin you notice "pavement plaques" that mark where things happened in the novel. One says, "He crossed at Nassau Street corner and stood before the window of Yeates and Son, pricing the field glasses." As the game of Monopoly is to Atlantic City, so is *Ulysses* to Dublin.

It was not June 16 when we were in Dublin, so I missed out on the literary magical mystery tour. I also missed out on the idea of using the novel as a directions device (I forgot too much). But we did visit the James Joyce Museum. It's near Dun Laughaire, walkable from anywhere in the city, and it's worth visiting for anyone with any interest in Ireland's most famous exile.

The mere existence of the museum says something about Ireland's "puzzle-the-world" contradictions. James Joyce was not, in life, a big fan of Ireland. Joyce described Ireland as (among other unpleasant things) "a Sow that eats its own farrow." If so, it never quite digested him. He also supposedly rejected Ireland's religion and even his own family. However, Ireland is, of course, the thing he always wrote about, from *Dubliners* on. It is quite remarkable to consider *Ulysses'* effect on Irish tourism. How many dollars have all these English majors tossed in on their yearly pilgrimages?

If Joyce is still floating around up there it's hard not to think that he would be astounded at the way things worked out. Writer rejects his country. He writes a book about Dublin. The book is declared obscene. The book is finally published. The "difficult" book becomes required reading in colleges everywhere in the English-speaking world. People who have read the book come back in droves to visit and leave money in the rejected country. Enough irony there.

Joyce's friend Oliver Gogarty felt that *Ulysses* became so big in America because Americans like crossword puzzles and detective stories and anagrams and smoke signals.

Whatever the reasons, no writer ever created a myth

around a city like Joyce, who said of his self-exile, "I go forth
to forge in the smithy of my soul the uncreated conscience of
my race." For Joyce, the ultimate player with words, the
word "forge," with all of its meanings, couldn't have been
accidental.

Ulysses is a great novel, but it's no good as directions-finder
in Dublin. We got in a cab and told the driver to take us to a
big American hotel. Hey, we were lost.

We woke up in a hotel in Dublin. It was our first non-B&B
night, and it was a little strange. There were no religious artifacts in the room, no holy water fonts, no crosses. There
was a picture on the wall. The frame looked more interesting
than the picture in it. It looked a little bit like a Chagall and
a little bit like a Picasso. It was color-coordinated with the
wallpaper. Our bed was huge and perfectly flat, the first perfectly flat bed we had slept in since we got to Ireland.

There was a huge dark brown piece of furniture with a
large television in it. Across the room there was a minibar.
Where the hell were we?

I flipped on the television. CNN. Augh. I flipped it off.

I went over and looked out the window. Yes, it was Ireland
all right. What now, room service?

I had been in hundreds of rooms like this in America, and
now, even though I was an ocean away, I was back in one.
Things started climbing the ladder of my consciousness. We
had checked into the hotel because we were tired and lost. I
was *still* tired. I had just completed, oh, nine hours of sleep,
but I found that I wanted a few more hours. But no. I drank
some coffee and got ready for another day in Ireland. It was
very odd in that hotel room. We were well rested and everything was nice, but it seemed that we were more in America
than in Ireland. I stumbled over to the shower.

I must admit that it was very comforting to experience
great water pressure again. After showers, we dressed, packed
our bags, and went down to eat breakfast.

Although it was on the menu, we didn't order the "Irish Breakfast." It didn't seem right to eat it in this huge room. I saw some people at a nearby table eating it, the same massive artery-clogger. The people eating it were wearing suits. One took a call while he was eating it. Cell phones and Irish breakfast? Blasphemy!

I listened to their voices. Yes, Irish people. But Irish people with yellow ties. The infamous Irish yuppies. I had heard of their existence but, up until now, I had thought them to be mythological. (I would see many more of them later.)

Paulette had a fried egg and bacon. I had cornflakes. I felt as Irish as Gorbachev.

We paid our bill and went to our car. We were feeling what Frank Kermode called "the Sense of an Ending." We knew that it was time to begin phase two of our Irish experience. Time to look for Mom and Dad.

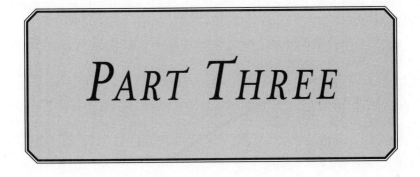

PART THREE

THIRTEEN

～ *Mom and Dad* ～

In 2002 most of the Irish people are in America. In 1841, the population of Ireland was 8,175,124. By 1926, the population sank to 4,228,553. During the years between 1841 and 1926, the world's population more than doubled. Ireland's numbers are a reminder of the enormous suffering the little country went through during those years. A lot of Irish people died, but a lot more left. And it is not inaccurate to say that today a large part of the Irish population is living in America.

The Irish started arriving in America in the 1820s. Economically, things were disastrous in Ireland, but they became much worse. The potato famine between 1845 and 1847 brought about one and a half million Irish people to America.

Most of the Irish people who left Ireland for America were, of course, poor. For the most part they stayed where their boat landed, New York, Boston, and, a little later, Chicago. Those three cities have massive Irish populations, but there are Irish people all over America. Montana, for instance, had a huge number of Irish immigrants.

According to the 1980 census, the Irish and their descendants form the third largest ethnic group in America. This massive exodus from Ireland has always produced big questions: Were the people who left Ireland castoffs, the dregs of society? Or were they actually the best of Ireland, the most ambitious: people whose aspirations could never be satisfied in their little homeland? These are impossible questions, but I know what my dad would say. For him, people who chose to live in a country like Ireland, when America was right here, merely three thousand miles away, were insane or lazy. For him, America saved him from a life of misery, working on a farm and living pretty much the way his people had lived for centuries. For a lot of Irish people, however, the rewards of the Old Country were more than enough, something they embraced and welcomed. There is something undeniably beautiful in the rural way of life in the West of Ireland; it's not something to be "saved" from.

In 1990 Mary Robinson, the president of Ireland, stated that there were 70 million Irish people living outside Ireland, most of them in the United States. So there is an Ireland that exists squarely in the United States, and it is much larger than the real Ireland. It is composed of people whose families had lived in Ireland for centuries, but now lived in America.

The list of Americans of Irish ancestry is pretty well-known, but some names still surprise. Buffalo Bill Cody. Butch Cassidy. William S. Hart. John Ford. Cardinal Spellman. Bill Murray. Jimmy Cannon. James Cagey. Bugs Moran. Grace Kelly. Nelly Bly. Jimmy Walker. Buster Keaton. John Huston. Bing Crosby. And on and on.

As the new century starts, Irish-Americans are, for the first time in history, going back to Ireland. This drastic change in the situation of the Irish-Americans is a nearly exact reversal of what has always been the pattern. While writing this book, I've met and talked to many people, some of them young and ambitious, whose parents had been born in Ireland. These people had been in America since birth, but now they were going back to live in Ireland on a permanent basis maybe eighty years after their parents "got off the boat." These people are dying to get back to Ireland, a country they see as an appealing place with a healthy and expanding economy.

Many first-generation Irish-Americans consider themselves (and their future) American. Most of these people visit Ireland a couple of times and nothing goes beyond that. They are born in America and they, along with their families, will die in America. They may root for Notre Dame. They may become members of some Irish organizations like the Hibernian Society. They may buy and read books about Ireland, but they never think of themselves as "Irish." I would have to fit in this category. I can't see Ireland getting so appealing that I go there permanently. Never say never, however.

There is no word in Irish for immigrant or emigrant. The Irish used the word "Jure," which really means "exile." "Immigrants" left their countries because they wanted to. The vast majority of Irish who left Ireland were leaving because they had to. That, more than anything else, is the Irish tragic moment: the beautiful, perfect place that you have to leave. Wakes are happy. Departures are sad.

Until fairly recently in Ireland the only economic factor was land. Since the English had permanently taken all the land, Irish people for centuries were faced with these options: A) Live in poverty and pay the English landlord; B) Make some weapons, band together, and then kill the English landlord; C) Leave. C was the popular choice—as an Irish person would say, the best of a bad lot.

You could go to England, the home of your oppressor, you could go to Australia, or you could go to America.

A lot of Irish mythology has to do with the ocean. The white tops of the waves are horses. There is a magic island out there, the land of eternal youth. Also, way way out there, is America. In the eighteenth century most of the people leaving Ireland for America were Protestants from the north. By the nineteenth century it was mostly Catholics. But reading about Ireland is reading about a departing. The songs about leaving and the songs about dying are the same songs.

Ellis Island is a couple of hundred yards north of the Statue of Liberty. Between 1892 and 1954 over ten million immigrants passed through there on their way into America. There is a good chance that if you are an American, your father or grandfather or great-grandfather or great-great-grandfather's first sight of America took place in Ellis Island.

Today there is a museum there. There are lots of artifacts and recorded oral histories and other mementos of coming into America. There is a big wall, the American Immigrant Wall of Honor, which contains the names of five hundred thousand immigrants. There's George Washington and Myles Standish. Nobody named Gannon up there.

My mom was twenty-three when she became a citizen of the United Stated on April 28, 1932. She listed her former nationality as "British," and her race as "Irish." When my dad became an American citizen, on January 11, 1935, he listed his former nationality as "British," but under race he wrote "_____."

This was not that surprising. My dad didn't like to draw attention to his Irishness. That was something that never changed with him. I have the documents.

My dad wrote my mom a letter on November 29, 1932. On December 22, 1945, he wrote her another letter. Between those two days my mom and my dad wrote a lot of letters. Herbert Hoover was president when the first letter was written. By the last, FDR had just died. The Great Depression ended between the letters, and World War II started and ended. The war ended, the letters stopped, my mom and dad got married, and, a few years later, I was born.

When my mom died I found the letters. They were kept neatly in a box with string around them. My mom must have kept almost all of my dad's letters. I couldn't find any that she wrote him. The letters my mom wrote would have been much longer. It was hard for me to picture my dad writing my mom a letter. It was hard for me to imagine him writing a letter to anybody. If he wrote the way he talked he would have done a lot better with postcards. Since a lot of the letters were written when my dad was in the army, I can see him stopping and asking the guys in the next bunk, "What can I say now?"

THE UNITED STATES OF AMERICA

No. 3856391

CERTIFICATE OF CITIZENSHIP

TO BE GIVEN TO
THE PERSON NATURALIZED

Petition No. 320

Personal description of holder as of date of naturalization: Age 26 years; sex Male color White
complexion Medium color of eyes Blue color of hair Brown height 6 feet 2 inches;
weight 185 pounds; visible distinctive marks None
Marital status Unmarried former nationality British

I certify that the description above given is true, and that the photograph affixed hereto is a likeness of me.

ORIGINAL

Bernard Gannon
(Complete and true signature of holder)

United States of America,
District of New Jersey, ss:

Be it known that BERNARD GANNON

then residing at 601 N. 2nd St., Camden, New Jersey
having petitioned to be admitted a citizen of the United States of America, and at
a term of the DISTRICT Court of THE UNITED
STATES held pursuant to law at
Camden, New Jersey on January 11th 1935

the court having found that the petitioner intends to reside permanently in the
United States (when so required by the Naturalization Laws of the United
States), and had in all other respects complied with the applicable provisions of
such naturalization laws, and was entitled to be so admitted, the court thereupon
ordered that the petitioner be admitted as a citizen of the United States of America.

In testimony whereof the seal of the court is hereunto affixed this 31st
day of January in the year of our Lord nineteen hundred and
thirty-five and of our Independence the one hundred
and fifty-ninth.

George T. Cranmer
Clerk of the U. S. District Court.

By Wm. A. Turner Deputy Clerk.

Seal

DEPARTMENT OF LABOR

THE UNITED STATES OF AMERICA

CERTIFICATE OF CITIZENSHIP

No. 3450944

TO BE GIVEN TO
THE PERSON NATURALIZED

Petition No. 3127

Personal description of holder as of date of naturalization: Age 23 years; sex Female color White
complexion Fair coloreyes Blue colorhair Black Height 5 feet 4 inches;
weight 118 pounds, visible distinctive marks None
race Irish former nationality British
Marital status Singlewoman

I certify that the description above given is true, and that the photograph affixed hereto is a likeness of me.

Miss Annie Forde

Anni Forde
(Complete and true signature of holder)

ORIGINAL

Seal

STATE OF PENNSYLVANIA) ss:
COUNTY OF MONTGOMERY)

Be it known that ANNIE FORDE
then residing at Mrs J. D. Winsor, Box 148, Haverford, Pa.,
having petitioned to be admitted a citizen of the United States of America and a
a term of the Regular Common Pleas
Montgomery County held pursuant to law at
Norristown, Pa., on April 28, 1932, 19

the court having found that the petitioner intends to reside permanently in the
United States had in all respects complied with the Naturalization Laws of the United
States in such case applicable, and was entitled to be so admitted, the court thereupon
ordered that the petitioner be admitted as a citizen of the United States of America.

In testimony whereof the seal of the court is hereunto affixed this 28th
day of April in the year of our Lord one thousand nine hundred and
Thirty Two (1932), and of our Independence the one hundred
and Fifty Sixth

Joseph V. Graham
Prothonotary or Clerk of the Common Pleas Court

By _____ Deputy Clerk.

I don't know what he did with her letters, but my dad moved around a lot when he was in the army, so maybe that's the reason. My mom had the same address throughout this period—Ardmore, Pennsylvania, where she worked for a rich, Mainline family, the Windsors. She helped out around their massive house, and she took care of the children. A lot of Irish girls did the same thing when they first came to America. A lot of them still do.

I was a little embarrassed for us when I found out that my mom had been a servant for over a decade. I first found this out when I was thirteen, an age when everything about your parents embarrasses you. My mom wasn't at all embarrassed. She was proud of the work she did. She called her job "nurse."

Because he was in the army when World War II started, my dad's letters were sent from all over Europe. It must have seemed ironic to him that he had tried so hard to get across the pond, and now they were sending him back. He never went to Ireland, although parts of England reminded him of the Old Country. He found France "about the same as Pennsylvania but not as nice as New Jersey."

The letters had a sort of tonal arc. He's depressed by the army, then bored, then interested but bored, then, as the war gets near its end, joyful and anticipatory. The last letters are very short—little notes more than letters, cut to fit into the V-Mail envelopes—and they all say pretty much the same things. The weather is good (or bad), he misses home, and he hopes that the war will be over soon. He played a lot of baseball with the division team and counted days.

But he didn't get to come home right away. He had to be in the Battle of the Bulge first.

When I was a kid I saw a movie called *The Longest Day*. It was a very famous movie starring almost every actor in Hollywood. I actually watched that movie all the way through. The movie gave the impression that after D-Day, the war was over and everybody could go home. That wasn't the truth.

The Battle of the Bulge was Germany's last big, all-out effort. Winston Churchill said that the Battle of the Bulge was "without any doubt, the greatest American battle of the Second World War." My dad, a guy who wasn't born in America and a guy who hated the army and enlisted only because he couldn't get a job during the Great Depression, a guy who, according to his letters, marked off the days until his discharge like a man in prison, wound up his military career in Belgium with 250,000 Nazis. During 98 percent of my dad's army tenure, the worst thing that happened happened in the mess hall. The food was lousy. The final 2 percent was a nightmare.

The death count in the Battle of the Bulge was amazing: Sixteen thousand Americans were killed. According to the records, a lot of them were, like my dad, first-generation Irish-Americans. They were fighting on the same side as England.

Adolf Hitler himself planned the Battle of the Bulge. Hitler, by December 1944, was a man with his back against the wall. Germany was clearly losing the war. The Russian Red Army was approaching from the east, while America was heavily bombing German targets. Italy had already been conquered, and the Allied armies were moving through France. My dad must have thought, rightly, that he was finally ending his hated army days.

But there was one thing left to do. The Battle of the Bulge. Germany's battle plan was to create a fifty-mile "bulge" in the Allied lines and penetrate to the Belgian port city of Antwerp. Most historians think Hitler knew he was a loser by this point, but he might have wanted to negotiate from strength and get a favorable peace settlement. If nothing else, if he was successful in what was called Wacht am Rhein, he would buy a little time.

The battle that ensued was the bloodiest battle in American history. Those sixteen thousand Americans were killed, but another sixty thousand were wounded. Hitler had a lot of his so-called "People's Infantry," which was composed of kids, the wounded, and basically anybody left in Germany. But he also had his elite Waffen SS, who were a trained veteran fighting force.

My dad found himself in a horrible position. He was in the group that was trapped around the town of Bastogne, surrounded and outnumbered by Nazi troops. The American situation was so perilous, the Nazis asked for surrender. General Tony McAuliffe, the American in charge, when asked to surrender responded in a famous manner: "Nuts!" he said.

The situation was so bad, Roosevelt actually thought about dropping the still unused atomic bomb. Eventually, America didn't have to use the bomb. The 101st Airborne Division was rushed in; they parachuted in a lot of supplies, and, eventually, they were able to drive the Germans back. Oddly, in driving them back, Americans lost more men than they had when they were under siege.

In what little I did hear of my dad's stories about the Battle of the Bulge, certain details stayed with me.

- My dad was operating a machine gun on a tripod. The guy who was supposed to be loading the long clips of bullets stopped. My dad started screaming at him. Then, out of the corner of his eye, my dad saw that the clip-loader had taken a bullet in his forehead and was lying on his side in the snow.
- My dad had three bullets hit his metal helmet within a few seconds. (He hated the army, but, he said, he had to admit they made good equipment and uniforms. My daughter Annie still wears one of his World War II coats. It hasn't lost a button.)
- In the cold, my dad found that he couldn't take his hands off the machine gun. When he did, he left a little skin on the gun controls.
- One guy had just entered the army three months ago. He didn't know what the hell he was doing. He was from

County Meath, near where my dad grew up. After they met, my dad and the guy talked for a long time about Ireland. The guy from County Meath got killed the very first day of action.

A pretty spotty picture is what I got of the Battle of the Bulge. I also have one other detail.

Once in a while, once every few months, my dad would wake up in the middle of the night. He would wake up in an extreme state of agitation and he would jump out of bed and crouch in the doorway to the bedroom. He would crouch there for a second, then he would get up and go back to bed. He didn't make a big deal out of this, and I wouldn't even know about it if my mom hadn't told me.

The first time it happened it was scary for her. After a few times, she said, she got used to it.

I asked her why he did that and she said she didn't know. She thought that maybe, back in the war, somebody bombed a house he was in and the only safe places were in the doorways.

I never asked him about it.

What would have happened if my dad had stayed in Ireland during World War II? Would he have gotten involved in the war anyway? In America, World War II is "the Good War," real bad guys against real good guys. There was no other choice: You had to take a side, and once you took a side, you were in the war.

I read a reprint of an article that was originally printed in 1941. It appeared in *The New Statesman* that year, and I think it states the true Irish position:

"The most seductive Englishman will fail to convince the most amenable Irishman that the Allies are fighting 'against aggression' and 'on behalf of democracy.' The British cause, to the Irishmen, is simply the patriotic cause of Britain, in which certain other countries have become involuntarily caught up through German invasion. It is not a cause whose nobility or whose claim on British lives Irishmen would dream of questioning. Nor do they criticize those of their own number who cross the border to enlist in the British Forces. But it is not a cause for which one Irish parent in a hundred will send his son to die; or one Irish voter in a hundred consent to plunge the country into war."

When he was old, when someone would ask my dad how he was doing, he wouldn't say "fine" or "good." He always said the same thing: "Getting through life with a minimum of difficulties."

FOURTEEN

～ *Dad* ～

My favorite American movie is pretty much the popular choice: *Citizen Kane.*

Citizen Kane still emotionally gets to almost everybody who watches it. I believe this is because everybody knows that they are, in a way, Charles Foster Kane. We are all enormous onions, complicated, almost but not quite comprehensible. We all walk around as these huge, multilayered onions. Sometimes, if we're lucky, we meet and fall in love with someone who wants to peel the onion all the way down to the core. Sometimes they get halfway in, discover a bad layer, and call off the project. Sometimes, with miraculous luck, we get someone who actually wants to go all the way into the giant Vidalia onion that is us. And we try to spend the rest of our lives with those people.

In my dad's own personal *Citizen Kane,* the word he whispers before dropping the glass snow sphere to the carpet and falling to the floor in death and eternal silence is one single, mysterious word: "Athlone."

Closeup on my dad's lips. No mustache.

"*Athlone.*"

My father was not very much like Charles Foster Kane. Bernard Gannon was a mysterious guy, though, a giant onion. He didn't live in a huge castle surrounded by wild animals, but he was a tough guy to figure out.

Athlone.

Two syllables. For all practical purposes, that was all I knew about my dad's youth. He was from some mysterious place in Ireland called "Athlone."

When I was a kid, I never wondered whether "Athlone" was a town, or a county, or a big city. It could have been a space station for all I cared.

"My dad's from Ireland," I would say.

Sometimes (rarely) the person I was talking to would ask, "Where at in Ireland?"

I would say, "Athlone." That was usually enough. The person I was talking to would cock his head as if he knew what I meant. Next question.

But the older I got, the more I wondered. I looked up "Athlone" in a book about Ireland. "Athlone" was a city near the middle of Ireland. From then on, when someone asked me about my dad, I would say, "My dad is from Ireland. From Athlone. That's a city near the middle of Ireland."

Then, when I was in college, my dad died and therefore closed his book permanently. At his funeral no one mentioned Athlone. Instead there was a lot of talk about Atlantic City and South Philly and East Camden.

My dad died in 1974, and since then the enigma of "Athlone" has grown in my mind. I got a picture book of Ireland out of the library and I looked at some pictures of Athlone. In the pictures, it looked like every other Irish town: freshly painted little shops that looked like they came out of 1920. Cobblestone streets. Kids with funny hats. Bicycles.

I consulted my atlas and found exactly where "Athlone" was. It turned out to be a little dot about 150 miles west of Dublin. So we expected to get to Athlone from Dublin by the afternoon. The drive is not particularly picturesque and we drove in silence, listening to the American top forty. We expected Athlone to be pretty much like the other Irish towns we had encountered, the two-pubs-a-pharmacy-and-some-bed-and-breakfasts town. It wasn't that way. Athlone, while not a metropolis, is actually much bigger than, say, Milltown Malbay or Ballyhaunis. Athlone is also a lot more modern. In some places Athlone could pass for the city my dad spent a lot more time in, Camden, New Jersey, the city of eternal love.

As expected we cruised into Athlone about lunchtime. We parked by the River Shannon, which flows through the center of Athlone. We got out of the Punta to explore a town we had heard of but never seen. When I was getting out of the car I almost tripped over a crushed sixteen-ounce Budweiser can lying on its side on the sidewalk. A group of multi-pierced young people walked past. They were listening to American rap music, something I hadn't missed up until now. It seemed pretty odd to be standing on a cobblestone street next to a river in Ireland listening to "All About the Benjamins."

A tall man in a thousand-dollar suit was walking along with a short man in a thousand-dollar suit. They were talking, but not to each other, muttering into their tiny black cell phones.

Almost immediately, Athlone started to transform us. As we talked, our answers got shorter and shorter. Athlone, against our wills, was turning us back into Americans. We might as well have been back there in the land of the free. We found ourselves acting what might be called "the American Way."

As we walked in our sullen way through the streets of Athlone, it was hard to imagine my dad as a kid hanging around in Athlone. I couldn't picture my dad walking around in an urban Ireland. Somehow it just didn't seem to ring true. But we were walking around in an urban Ireland, and it wasn't doing us any good. It wasn't killing us, but it wasn't doing us any good.

I started to hear some music from a store, drifting out in front. The Boss. "The Streets of Philadelphia." It seemed to be almost appropriate. Then we happened to pass a store. There was a big sign over the door: GANNON'S.

Paulette didn't want to go inside. She felt we should keep walking. I thought that I had to try Gannon's. Actually, I was looking for a little "meditation time." I went in alone.

It was empty except for a young man behind the counter. I looked him over. He was about twenty-five. He was an inch or so shorter than I was, about my weight. He was a round-faced, clean-shaven, red-haired, friendly sort of guy. He looked really Irish. Duh.

"Can I help you?" he said.

"Yes." I started on my stumbling introduction. I was from America. My name was Frank Gannon. I knew that my father had grown up around Athlone. His name was Bernard Gannon. He was born in 1908. He lived near Athlone until he was about twenty. Then he went to America. That's about it. Could he help me?

I can't remember the man's first name, but his last name was Gannon, which was comforting. He didn't know whether he could help me. He called into the back room. An older man came out. He looked like a man who had just woken. I told him my story. He shook hands with me. He paused and looked puzzled.

One of the Gannons said, finally, "I have some people for you to meet."

He motioned for me to follow him.

I followed him down a narrow hallway. There was a sort of living room back there. There were chairs and a rug and a re-frigerator and a television. It looked like the set for a sitcom. There were several people sitting around drinking and watching television. Mr. Gannon introduced me to a young woman and an older woman and a heavy man in his sixties and a tall skinny man in his thirties. They gave me a drink. I tasted it. It was whiskey. It tasted very good.

I got introduced to everybody. He said the name of the person, and then he said, "This is Frank Gannon." He said it as if it meant something. And the person who was named

"Gannon" acted as if he or she was very pleased to be meeting Frank Gannon.

"Frank Gannon," they'd say. They smiled warmly and shook my hand.

I drank the whiskey and talked. Everybody was very friendly. We laughed and talked about this and that. It soon became clear, however, that I wasn't related, even faintly, to anyone in the room. I wasn't even possibly anybody's third cousin twice removed.

I was just some guy who wandered in off the street.

But we still had a nice talk. I finished my drink. They offered me another, or maybe some tea. I said I had to be going. How about a scone? No, I can't. Are you sure? They're very good. Nice and hot. Fresh-baked. No, no, I can't, sorry. We have a busy day planned.

I said my goodbyes, walked to the front of the store, opened the door, and walked into the sunny day.

Paulette was standing there. Her arms were folded in front of her. She was not happy. I had been in there almost twenty minutes. We started walking.

"Well," she said, "what happened?"

"Nothing," I said.

We walked along and, for the next twenty minutes, neither of us uttered a single syllable. But I felt a little better.

We wandered around for a while. Then we went where all confused people in Ireland have traditionally gone: to the Catholic church.

There are two huge Catholic churches in Athlone: Saint Peter's and Saint Mary's. Saint Peter's was the first church we came across. I opened the door and we walked inside.

Saint Peter's was quite a place. It was a beautiful, huge, elaborate church with amazing stained-glass windows and polished marble and beautifully carved wood everywhere and soaring ceilings and startling, elaborate gold tabernacles. It was completely empty except for one little guy who was kneeling in a back pew all alone. He turned around and noted our presence, then turned back to his praying.

Paulette and I tentatively made our way up to the altar. We went in different aisles because we were still in the midst of the aforementioned American-Alienation-Athlone experience. Our steps echoed in the huge space as we made our desultory way up our separate aisles. I looked over and saw that she was a little in front of me, so I started to walk faster. She saw me inching ahead and increased her speed. Although she was in better aerobic shape than I, I am bigger. My stride is longer. I tried to get to the altar first, and I barely made it, beating her by about two lengths. I looked at her smugly. I could see she was "less than thrilled."

I was very happy to notice that there was a woman in back of the altar. She had been invisible from the rear of the cavernous church when we entered. She stopped what she was doing and turned. Our eyes met.

"Excuse me," I said. I began my pathetically lame, stumbling spiel. It was slightly more fluid because of the whiskey back in Gannon's. I started to think, wistfully, of Gannon's. Maybe I should go back there. I was liked and respected there. I was an "insider."

The woman turned around. I had been using the time-tested stare-at-the-back-of-the-person's-head-until-they-turn-around method.

"I don't know if you can help me, but I'm from America and I'm over here looking into my father's past because he was born here in Ireland but he later moved to America, where I was born, and I just wondered whether you could help me find out anything about his life over here in Ireland before I was born . . . "

I paused and noticed that my words were having absolutely no effect. Was it possible that she was not an English-speaking person? In the middle of Ireland, it seemed very unlikely that she could be a non-English-understanding person. Maybe it was just my American accent. Or maybe (which seemed like the best bet) I was just being really lame.

I paused again. The silence in the big church was very heavy. It made me a little nervous. When I get nervous, I have a tendency to babble, so I started to babble again.

"So they always say, in America, that if you are really confused about something and you are in Ireland, the best place to go is a church . . . " I looked at the lady. She didn't think my "church" comment was amusing. As a matter of fact, she looked as if she found me both unamusing and stupid. I looked over at Paulette. She looked just like the lady. They could be bookends.

The lady spoke. Her voice was very flat and emotionless, like someone announcing train schedules.

"Sir," she said, "I'm the florist."

She went back to her flowers. I thought *Well, the fact that you're the florist doesn't mean you can't be helpful.*

At that point, Paulette walked away. Great move, babe. Then I realized that she had seen someone, another lady, in the little room behind the altar. This lady looked like someone who knew what was going on. I followed Paulette, who didn't acknowledge that act in any perceptible way.

When I walked into the room, the lady was looking through a shelf of books. These were major-league books. They were bound in red leather and they looked big enough to contain all known Irish knowledge. Each one of the books was thicker than a Manhattan white pages. The lady removed one of the books from the shelf. She brought it over and plopped it on a table. This was a strong woman. The thing must have weighed thirty-five pounds.

The big red book turned out to be a computer-generated list of everyone who had ever had anything to do with Saint Peter's of Athlone: their birth, baptism, First Holy Communion, wedding, divorces (a decidedly un-Catholic-Irish bit of information), all of their addresses, their death, and, in bold computer print, their yearly contributions to Saint Peter's, before and after death. I was wondering how they could give money *after* they were dead. Did someone give it in their name? What's the point there? Does the dead guy want a tax deduction? A big computer-generated page always makes me start thinking like that.

The big red book consisted, I noticed with quiet amazement, of just the letters "G," "H," and "I." A thirty-five-pound book. They kept good records here at Athlone. I had thought it was a sleepy little hamlet, but it was really data headquarters, Ireland central.

But there was absolutely nothing in the big red book about Bernard Gannon. There were a few Bernard Gannons, but not *the* Bernard Gannon. Not the Bernard Gannon with enormous hands. Not the Bernard Gannon who had left Athlone and sailed to America and married Anne Forde and had several children, one of whom was a remarkable literary figure who was really good sexually and a credit to his race.

When we walked out of the church the little guy with the bulbous nose was still there praying. He looked at me. He looked as if he felt sorry for me.

After that, the afternoon turned fouler and fouler and testier and testier, as did the general mood. We started walking a few steps apart. It was slowly becoming one of those afternoons that are best erased from the memory bank. I had experienced a thousand afternoons like that, but this was the first in Ireland.

Finally I stopped, excused myself, and went and got an ice cream cone. That, oddly, was the last straw. When I returned to Paulette, slurping my cone (very good butter pecan in a sugar cone, by the way), things got ugly.

"You *had* to get that, didn't you?"

"No," I said, reaching back for my reserve sarcasm, "I didn't *have* to do that. I *chose* to do that." I knew I was fanning the flames, but I was far beyond caring.

Now we walked along in sullen silence. Blocks of Ireland

were passed without comment. I thought, randomly, that it reminded me, somehow, of the Newark airport.

Finally, after a sullen eternity, we got to our tiny automobile, our wretched Punta. Paulette got in what would be, in America, the passenger door, a sign that she desired to drive. I was in no mood to say otherwise. We drove out of Athlone. "I got the music in me," was playing on the radio.

The traffic, as you would figure, was terrible. It started to rain. I looked at the guy in the car next to us. He looked as if he belonged on the New Jersey Turnpike. People were honking their horns and passing on the impossibly narrow streets. Paulette got a little too close to the curb and severely mangled a hubcap.

Somehow, as it was interpreted, the mangling was all my fault. I welcomed the responsibility. Mangle the other one, woman. I'll take the blame for that one too. When someone blamed my mother for something that wasn't her fault, she always said, *Go ahead, put it on me. I've got broad shoulders.*

I didn't say that to Paulette but I was thinking it.

Now things got ugly. The horrible weather (it started, on cue, to pour, the first hard rain we had seen in Ireland). The terrible, aggressive Athlone drivers. The sullen florist. The bitter ice cream cone purchase. The mangled hubcap.

Silence fell.

Ireland sucks, I thought.

We drove like statues in the front seat of our tiny red car to an Irish Heritage Center, the sort of remote outpost that desperate, suicidal tourists seeking their ancestral roots go in times of desperate need.

The Irish Heritage Center was an ugly, squat, white brick building set in an unpromising empty lot. It had a sign that advertised lessons in traditional "Riverdance" stepping. Sure, stop here. This is the right place for our foul, nihilistic mood. No place could be better. Let's all riverdance. I can be lord of the motherless dance. I'm a Mick. Bite me.

Soon, I thought, there may be gunplay. In a final confrontation between Paulette and me, I felt that I would emerge triumphant. I was much larger and I felt confident that, if it came to it, I would prove to be the better man.

The last act of *La Boheme* is cheerier than the mood we brought with us to the Irish Heritage Center. But it was there that things, blissfully and surprisingly, started to look up. The lady at the Heritage Center listened to our story about looking for my dad's roots. Her eyes said that she had heard this story many, many times, and the last time was ten minutes ago. She gave us a form, told us where to send it, told us what it would cost in American dollars to do a computer check on all the Gannons in the area, yadda, yadda, and was about to bid us goodbye. I was thinking about the desultory road back to Athlone. I asked myself, "What would Samuel Beckett do?"

Then the heritage lady furrowed her brow. She raised her chin slightly.

"So the name is Gannon?" she asked.

"Yes," I said, "and Turley." Turley was my grandmother's maiden name, a fact I picked up from a trip to the Mormon website.

"You know, there's an old gent a few miles from here, Noel Turley. And I believe there's some Gannon in him. Let me give you directions."

It was hard to believe. Something not completely bad.

We drove down a little road: a left turn from the road to Moate, a village about ten miles from Athlone. The houses were few and far between, but they were pretty nice houses. It looked as if some of them were larger, renovated versions of the *Quiet Man* house, with the thatched roof replaced with slate.

We drove past an old man in a suit. We stopped.

"Excuse me, sir," I asked. "Do you know Noel Turley?"

"Noel Turley?" he said. He said it as if shocked that I would ask him such an obvious question.

"He's about five kilometers away. There's an old caved-in-house, and a railroad, and a new house. Turley's in the new house."

Now we were cooking. We drove along happily, the misery of Athlone happily beginning to crumble. It stopped raining. The sun, a rare thing in Ireland, started to peep through the gray clouds. Our bleak Samuel Beckett afternoon mood was slowly beginning to dissipate.

We passed a caved-in house. I didn't notice a railroad. There was an old gent with a friendly looking red face. He was stumbling in his yard. There was something mysteriously familiar about him. We stopped the car.

"Excuse me, do you know Noel Turley?" I asked.

"Speaking," he said.

Noel Turley invited us in and we walked into his house. He acted as if we lived next door and had last visited the house yesterday. He introduced us to his wife, who was very gracious and friendly. Noel directed us to our seats. We sat down in his living room. Yes, he had holy water fonts.

Noel Turley, it turned out, was related to me in some obscure way, but it was such a complex, tangled line of aunts, and cousins, and grandmothers, that I cannot say exactly what that way was without consulting sources. I can diagram it more easily than I can explain it. But, after talking with Noel for a while, it really felt as if I knew him, as if I had known him for a very long time, since I was a kid. He seemed as if he had been at all those Saint Patrick's Day Hibernian parties at my cousin's restaurant.

Noel Turley knew a great deal about the Gannons. He knew all three of the brothers, Bill Gannon, Johnny Gannon, and my dad, Bernie Gannon. Johnny was the character, but Bernie was the tough one. He told me a little story about my dad and some potatoes. This is a story that depended a lot on the performance, but it was, told by Noel, a great story, but an Irish story without a plot. I had heard many of them from my mother. I thought that it is a great tale, but essentially un-repeatable because it depends more on the performance than the details. Anyway, here it is, sans performance.

"I had some spuds. And this man told me to sell 'em. I asked him, 'Are they good?' and he said, 'They're fair.' Now 'fair' isn't 'good.' It's worse than good. So 'fair' is another way of saying 'bad.' So I tasted one. And it was worse than 'bad.' You'd do better eating the dirt it grew in. So I was walking around with the sack of spuds, and I saw your dad. And I knew he was headed off to America in a few days. And I asked him to sell the spuds for me. And he said, 'Are they good?' And I said, 'They're fair.' So I went off to mass. When I came back I saw Bernie. And the spuds weren't with him. And I asked him if he sold them. He said, 'I did.' And I said, 'Who did you sell them to?' And he said, 'A lady.' And I split the money with him. And I asked him, 'Do you know what "fair" means?' And he said, 'I think it means "bad." ' And I said, 'Do you know the lady?' And he said, 'I do.' And I said, 'What are you going to tell her when she sees you again?' And he said, 'When she sees me again, I'll look different.' And then he went to America."

Noel took me on an amazing tour of the world my dad saw when he first saw the world. The house my dad was born in was still standing, sort of. Next to it was a little barn, which was also still standing. Sort of. My dad's place was six acres. They didn't "own" the land. They "rented" it from some-body they rarely saw. It looked impossible to farm.

They did farm it. It was almost a living when everyone was alive. You ate what you grew. It is the sort of place that looks beautiful in a photo, but would be mind-numbingly hard to work. They got by until the bad things happened.

Noel then showed me the cemetery that he thought some of my people might be buried in. This was within easy walk-ing distance. Noel was an easy man to talk with. If you couldn't think of anything to say, no problem. Talking was like shooting a water pistol standing in a lake. There were no Pinteresque moments.

We finally came to the cemetery. It was very small, a square twenty feet on a side. There were maybe ten graves there. A lot of the writing on the tombstones was worn away, but right in the front I saw it. The grave of the grandpa I never saw. I never heard my father talk about him.

JOSEPH GANNON
DIED MARCH 15, 1916, AGED 45 YEARS

And under that.

FRANCIS GANNON
BELOVED SON
DIED DECEMBER 21, 1916

Francis was the brother I was named after.

So my dad was seven years old when his dad died and eight when his big brother died. Bernie was eight years old, but he was the man of the house. He had to start making a living. On six "leased" rocky acres in Ireland. He quit school and worked.

I asked a few questions and tried to put together something like my dad's typical day when he was very young. He had told me that he had always worked, that he had been forced to quit school when he was a little kid. He would get up early and take the horse out. He would walk from farm to farm, attempting to get a farmer interested in sort of "renting" the horse for a day. When my dad did get somebody interested, he would stick around and help him hitch up the horse and plow.

When he got home, he wasn't finished yet. As the man of the house, he had to do most of the chores as well as help look after his little brothers and sister. He would fall into his bed hungry, tired, and sore. Tomorrow he would get up and do it again. And again.

I looked again at the little house with the caved-in room. At the thick walls. I looked out the window, the view my dad saw every morning. I remember some few comments that my dad did make about those years. "The animals got fed better than I did." "We didn't have enough money to be poor." I realized why he didn't laugh when he said those things.

I thought of looking at my old man sleeping on the beach in Ocean City, New Jersey. I remember, as a little kid, being amazed at all the little scars all over his back and legs. I remember looking at his huge hands, how his fingernails were all broken. I remember asking him how they got that way. I remember him telling me that I didn't want to know.

And I understood why my dad mowed down my tomato plants.

The greatest Irish play may be *The Playboy of the Western World*. The theme of the play is a very familiar Irish motif: The son, to earn the respect of both himself and those around him, must, in some way, symbolic or literal, kill the father.

I have written a lot of boxing journalism, and I vividly remember an old trainer telling me, "Irish fighters? Their first go is always their old man."

I could never imagine hitting my dad, but I guess, in some subconscious Freudian way, I saw him as a rival for my mom. This whole thing remained subliminal, but I do remember the quiet satisfaction I took in showing him how much better I was at certain sports than he could ever be. Of course he never saw a basketball until he was in his thirties, and he was utterly clueless at golf (we played once) and bowling (we played many times). I do remember sitting there watching him sit in his big chair reading his newspaper, and I remember thinking, after he punished me for something, *I will do things that you can't do, old man.*

So I guess he was, on some Oedipal level, the guy I had to overcome. I remember one incident that seemed to encompass all this.

I had just come home from college. I was twenty. I weighed 205. I was "almost as big as your old man" to guys at the bar. (I worked on vacations.) I had lifted weights every day for about a year. My dad and I sat alone at our kitchen table. We had consumed two or three beers. No one was anywhere near drunk, but I felt a little buzzed. I don't know how it started, but we decided to arm wrestle.

His hand was like a catcher's mitt with calluses. He was, at that point, over sixty. He was wearing bifocals. We began.

It took about five minutes. I won. I was not surprised. I had won my dormitory bench press contest. I could bench 325. I was a very dangerous person. I had menacing veins.

He stood up and walked to the refrigerator. He came back with two long-neck bottles of Budweiser. I tried to be graceful in victory. Yeah, Dad, you're really strong for your age. I've been working out a lot.

Near the end of the beer he wanted to try it again. I rolled my eyes a little. Sure. Why not? I won't rub it in. But I would not, I firmly decided, lose. No way.

It took less than thirty seconds. I never had a chance. He had gotten a lot stronger since the walk to the kitchen. My hand hurt. I felt like saying, "No fair!" but I couldn't think of anything to claim. I felt like my shoulder was dislocated. I had that injury before and now I had it again.

He went to bed.

My dad died on June 2, 1974. He died from cancer. He knew he had cancer for several years but he didn't do anything to treat it. At his funeral I asked an old friend if my dad had said anything when he found out he had cancer. He could remember my dad saying only one thing: "That figures."

He died at home. The last time I saw him, he weighed

about 170 pounds. My dad's bones probably weighed 160. He rolled up his sleeve, looked at his thin yellowish arm, and said, "I can't believe that's my arm." He shook his head and stared straight ahead.

"Me," he said. "I can't get used to this."

At his wake a lot of people that I didn't know showed up. Some of them told stories about how my dad kicked various people's asses. Two old guys discussed how far he threw a guy out of his bar.

He was buried in a cemetery across the street from where we went bowling. He was an inconsistent bowler. He'd bowl 250 and then bowl 120. He was the only person I ever saw who used a bowling ball with only two holes. Two big holes.

"That's best for me," he told me.

My dad's funeral was held on a very sunny day. Then we drove in the hearse to the graveyard. On the way over someone made a joke. We laughed politely.

We got out of the hearse and stood around in our black clothes and sunglasses. While the priest read the "Thou art ashes" part, I thought about how, when we rode past the cemetery after work, he would say the same lame joke.

"That's the most popular place in town. People are dying to get into it."

He told me that about fifty times—every time there was somebody else in the car with us.

My cousin Bill, the only priest in the family, read the service. My mom always wanted me to be a priest. She wanted my brother Bud to be a priest. Bud got a lot closer, but we didn't make it.

She didn't look at Bill while he read. She didn't look at me. She didn't look at my dad's casket. She looked at the parking lot. At the end I walked over to my mom. I didn't know what to say. She looked at me.

"Are you hot?" she asked.

FIFTEEN

~ *Mom* ~

We awoke in our larger-than-usual bed and breakfast room in a place just outside Athlone. I looked around the room and decided to count the religious artifacts in the room. There were nine, not counting the cross over the other side of the door.

This seemed like a good jumping-off point for our search for Mom.

Athlone is about fifty miles due west from my mom's home. So, after the massive breakfast, we knew that we wouldn't be driving more than an hour or two. The day was pretty clear (by Irish standards). The Punta had a little minor dent on one of the wheel covers (a by-product of Athlone), but otherwise it was still capable of attaining the mind-jarring speed of forty-five miles per hour, and we were in no big hurry. We had a lot more information about my mom. Compared to the Athlone search, this was going to be easy.

We had, of course, been very near "Mom Land" earlier in our trip. But on our way back out to the west, we intentionally meandered even more than our usual meandering. No matter where you drive in the West of Ireland, you feel you were somehow meant to go there. If you make some wrong turns they aren't really wrong.

They Love Their Mothers

John Belushi did a great little bit where he pretended to be a straight-arrow newsperson. He began, "Well the calendar says March 17, and we all know what that means. It's the time everybody is a little bit Irish. It's the time for 'the wearin' of the green.'" He then continued in that same, standard television announcer's voice, saying the same boring clichés you hear every Saint Patrick's Day. "Top o' the morning," "Sure and begorrah," "The luck of the Irish," ad nauseum.

Then he said, "I know this guy, he's Irish. He's a friend of mine. I hadn't heard from him in a couple of years, but he gives me a call, wants me to pick him up at the airport." Belushi then told us about the Irish guy, who was a crazy drug dealer. Belushi's voice became more and more manic as he told about his "friend" and his efforts to smuggle serious narcotics into the country. As he told the lurid story, Belushi got more and more out of control. Finally he was standing screaming about his crazy Irish friend. The bit ended with Belushi completely spinning out and falling to the ground.

I found this bit so funny I found it in a rental place (it's on *The Best of John Belushi*). I play it as part of my traditional Saint Patrick's Day celebration right before the eatin' of the corned beef. But the interesting thing is the last words Belushi spits out before collapsing: "Oh, they love their mothers!"

I never met an Irish guy who didn't love his mother. I love my mother. I've never met anyone quite like her. If that sounds a little Oedipal, well, too bad. I can honestly say that I never saw my mom do or say anything that was in any way "wrong." I mean that in a moral sense. In the other senses of the word, she was always doing something "wrong."

She went to mass every day of her life. In the evenings she

prayed for a couple of hours. I vividly remember a scene from her life. It was pure Anne Forde.

I was about twelve years old. I was with my mom and dad and my brother and sister. We were at the racetrack. Delaware Park, about an hour from our house, was the only racetrack that admitted children. My dad would let me pick horses. If I won he would give me the money. It was a fun day. It probably wasn't the most psychologically healthy thing to let a little kid bet on horses, but I loved it. I never said we were the Waltons. (I never became a compulsive gambler, but I love horse racing.) The racetrack was, for us, "family entertainment." The family that gambles together, stays together.

Anyway, my dad was having a bad day. My mom was having a good day. My mom never bet more than two dollars, while my dad frequented the hundred-dollar window. On a bad day, my mom would lose maybe twenty dollars. My dad would lose serious Benjamins. My mom always smiled and laughed and made jokes no matter how she was doing. My dad's disposition depended on his economic state; on a bad day he was not Mister Rogers.

It was late afternoon. The eighth race of the day had just finished. My dad had not been at the winner's window all afternoon. He was less than thrilled. In the race that had just finished my mom's horse acted up in the starting gate and was scratched. This meant that everyone who had bet on that horse would get his money back. But that's all. If you bet ten bucks you would get ten bucks back. My mom had just returned from the window. She looked puzzled. She sat down next to my dad, who was wearing an intense fixed stare. He was looking at nothing, something he did when things weren't going well.

My mom told my dad her problem. She had gone to the window to get her two dollars back, but the guy at the window had given her a lot more than two dollars. He had made a mistake and given her the payoff for the winning horse, a long shot that paid sixty-two dollars. The racetrack had just given my mom sixty dollars.

This news lightened my dad's mood. I could see a little twinkle in his eyes. I could almost read his thoughts. Sixty dollars. Not bad. The racetrack just gave us sixty dollars. Life is not that bad.

Then my mom said something that completely shattered his mood.

"I'm going back to give the money back." And with that, she was gone. I looked over at my dad. I could just make out some steam coming from his ears.

My mom hadn't even thought about keeping the money. That was the way she was with everything. Once she went way out of her way to return a twenty-five-cent pencil she had inadvertently stuck in her purse. She probably spent fifteen dollars giving back the pencil. The Ten Commandments were, for her, not the "Ten Suggestions."

My mother told me that when she was a young girl she had a powerful desire to become a nun. She told me that she believed that God had chosen her. She set out to begin her training three separate times, and three times something happened that prevented her from going. Sometimes someone got sick and she was needed at home. Sometimes someone got in an automobile accident. My mom interpreted that as God's way of telling her that she wasn't meant to be a nun.

But for my mom, the next best thing would be to be the mother of a nun or, better, a priest. I never really felt her directing me toward the priesthood. I guess there was something about me that just said, "Not priest material." But my older brother received the full treatment. It didn't take. It didn't work with my sister Mary either. (She would have been a really aggressive nun.)

There were always priests around the house when I was growing up. Some of them I liked and some of them I did not. I now know that they were there to show my brother what the life of a priest was like. If the priests at our house were typical, the priestly life didn't look that bad. They all had cars. Some of them drank a little, some smoked, but none of them had any sexual predilection for young boys. I mention that only because of recent events, but for years before that, every time you saw an actor playing a priest he was a child molester. I was an altar boy for seven years and I never saw anything remotely sexual.

I really enjoyed being an altar boy. You got to dress up in exotic clothing. You got to set fire to a lot of stuff (candles, incense, once in a while the exotic clothing). But the one thing I remember most about being an altar boy is a fellow altar boy I will call Tommy Ditmar.

Ditmar was about three years older than I was, so I got to observe his altar boy career for about three years. I guess he was my role model in the religious life. He was an older and wiser altar boy. He was a tall wiry kid with large hands and crazy hair. His hair looked as if Ditmar had just stuck his hand in an electrical socket. The hair was appropriate. Ditmar was not the model altar boy.

He would do the usual altar boy bad stuff (sword fights with the candle lighters), but he went way beyond that. He would wait until the priest was gone. He would make sure of Father Bradley's absence and then go into his act.

First he would go over to the refrigerator and get out a bottle of Christian Brothers wine, the wine used in the mass. I was stunned that he had the brass to do that. He would walk around taking gulps out of the bottle while engaging in a stream-of-consciousness monologue that was really, really obscene and really, really anti-Catholic (anti-everything was closer to it). For my ten-year-old mind it was the funniest thing I ever heard. While he was doing this, striding around, pretending he was the bishop or the pope, he would continually munch on a stack of communion wafers.

I remember being really shocked the first time I saw Ditmar's act. The wafers were, after all, sacred, and here was

Tommy Ditmar buying himself a one-way, no-waiting ticket to hell.

He always ended his rant the same way. He would say something really filthy and anti-God. Then, while everyone was laughing (usually an audience of two or three other altar boys), he would plop into the big red chair that they had in the corner of the sacristy, the one underneath the somber portrait of Pope Pius XII. Ditmar, really rolling now, would take a huge slug of Christian Brothers, clap his hands, and say in a loud, booming voice, a voice like the voice of God in the movies (or as close as Ditmar could get), "Bring me the dancing girls!"

Ditmar's performances burned themselves into the template of my mind. Whenever I see an altar boy, I think of him and smile. Whenever I see an altar boy, I think of Ditmar, the chair, and the dancing girls.

I didn't become a priest. Sorry, Mom. I blame Ditmar.

I did not know Tommy Ditmar. I saw him only "on duty." Someone told me that he became a full-fledged substance abuser. I can only think of him in a big red chair with a bottle of Christian Brothers in his hand and a wild maniacal grin on his face.

I am very happy that my mother never saw one of Ditmar's performances. For her, the Catholic Church was the holiest of places, and all the altar boys were like little angels on earth. My mother grew up on a farm outside a little town in County Mayo named Ballyhaunis. (There are many little towns in Ireland that begin with "Bally.") Like "Athlone," this was, for me, merely a couple of syllables with no meaning. She never talked enough about it to give me a mental picture of Ballyhaunis. When we got an "official" Basset hound and needed an official registered "last name" for the low-IQ dog, we named it "Norman O'Ballyhaunis."

He later drank antifreeze and died. It was very sad. We all really loved him. Norman wasn't too swift in the brain department, but he was very lovable. He had an Irish name, so it is appropriate that he died because he was too fond of drinking.

As far as my consciousness goes, that is the only real "Ballyhaunis" connection that I have ever had. This seems horrible to me now, but when I was younger I was not at all interested in my mom's Irish life. I was extremely close to my mother, but she rarely talked about her life back in Ireland. If she wanted me to know, I figured, she would have told me about it.

In the DNA department I'm pretty momlike. When I was born, she told me, my relatives said that I resembled my mother's side of the family. They said, many, many times in my presence "He's a Ford, not a Gannon." When Gerald Ford said that he was a Ford, not a Lincoln, I was repulsed for a variety of reasons. My dad would stand no Republican associations, however remote.

I have my dad's weird curly hair, and I'm almost as big as he was. But from the wrist down I'm all Anne Forde's son. My mother had tiny hands. They looked almost comical next to my dad's Sonny Liston hands. I am six-foot-two, but my hands wouldn't look out of place on Michael J. Fox. I used to be very self-conscious about the size of my hands. When I was in high school my friend George Bianchi said that I was the only kid in his high school who needed two hands to play Monopoly.

I, like most American boys, once had a gripping desire to dunk a basketball. I was six-two—I should be able to dunk. I played a lot of basketball, and my nondunker status was kind of embarrassing. I could jump high enough, but I would always lose the ball on the way up. I could dunk a volleyball, but my hands were too small for a one-hand dunk with a basketball, and I couldn't jump high enough for a two-hand dunk. This used to frustrate me. I once tried gluing the ball to my hand with LaPage's Mucilage. This resulted in my injuring myself. The ball stuck to my hand when

I tried to "dunk," and I dislocated my shoulder. When I told the doctor how I injured myself he looked at me like, "This boy is really unusually stupid."

Anne Forde's chromosomes also got to me in more subtle ways. I loved to sit around and talk to my mom. Unlike my dad she would talk back to me. I certainly inherited a lot of her personality. I, like the pants at a liquidation mart, have always been "slightly irregular." I never quite fit in. I felt as if I was the same type of person as my mother—not criminal, just sort of confused on some level.

My mom had a very strange sense of humor, which I find very difficult to describe. When she told jokes, she always told them very badly. She went on past the punch line, or she forgot something, or she added odd details that didn't add anything, or she grafted another joke on to the original joke.

Then she would laugh at the wrong moment. She would laugh at her strange version of the joke, not the joke. Sometimes, in a very strange way, her little addition to the joke *was* funnier. I would sometimes laugh in the middle of her joke. I'd realize that I had laughed at the wrong time. Then I would look at her and her eyes would say, "I meant to do it that way."

She would tell the same joke differently every time. If my mom asked, "Have you heard this one?" the answer was always, "No," because no one had ever heard it because no one had ever told it. And no one would ever tell it again.

I found that I usually laughed at my mother's jokes. Often, no one else did. A bond was formed, a bond more basic than the mother-son relationship, the bond of weirdness.

My mom and I would go to the movies all the time. We would get a cab because she didn't drive. Someone (not my dad) once tried to teach her. She described to me her one driving lesson. She sat in the driver's seat. She put it in reverse. She tried to get out of the driveway. She didn't make it. She gave up.

In the taxi, she would sit in the backseat and I would al-

ways want to sit in the little fold-down seat that yellow cabs
had back then. I thought it was interesting to unfold the little fold-down seat they had in front of the rear seating area.
It made me feel that I was doing something intricate and important.

So, I'd be facing my mom as we rode into Philadelphia.
My mom would talk to the cab driver, but I could tell that
she was also talking to me. She was right in front of me.

My mom loved to talk. She would start talking in a rhyth-
mic, rambling Irish voice the moment she got into the cab,
and she wouldn't stop until we got there. The cab drivers
were usually good talkers too. I could tell that they enjoyed
giving a long five-dollar ride to a talker of this quality. The
cab drivers had their themes. They often complained about
Philadelphia and the plight of cabdrivers. My mom sympa-
thized. Sometimes I would make an observation. She would
weave my comment into the conversation so I felt I was engaging in an actual grown-up conversation. My observations
were always quickly dismissed, but I was in there conversing.

She loved baseball and she would talk about the Phillies in
great, almost baroque detail. This was often startling to people who didn't know her. She did not look like a person who
would have a Red Barber–like view of the game.

When I told friends that my mom knew about baseball,
they always got the wrong idea. If my friend was over at my
house, and didn't know my mom, he might ask her something like, "How are the Phillies, Mrs. Gannon?"

This was like asking Alan Dershowitz, "How is the law?"

My mom wouldn't say "good" or "bad," as my friend
would expect. She would say something like, "Gene Mauch
doesn't use his bullpen enough." Or, "They have to get a
right-handed pinch hitter, a power hitter if he's available, because in the late innings every team in the National League
has a left-handed relief guy, and the Phillies can't do anything
at that point." Or, "When Tony Gonzalez got hurt, they let

everybody pitch around Callison. They should move him up in the order. He can bat second. He is a good contact hitter."

My mom knew more about baseball than my friends. She also knew more than I did. That's because she listened to the Phillies games with rapt, focused attention.

When I got older, I wondered about this. Since she was, after all, from Ireland, where baseball was not played, and none of her friends (or her husband) were at all interested in baseball, I found her interest puzzling.

She told me about her introduction to the game, her first impressions. At her first game she was astounded, like so many other people, upon entering the stadium and seeing the vast green in the middle of the dingy gray city of Philadelphia, in the dingy gray area of Twenty-first and Lehigh Avenue. Almost every baseball fan I know, however, has that same impression imprinted on his or her brain. What else?

She told me that she was astounded at the fact that a long towering fly ball to center field was just an out, while a tiny, off-the-end-of-the-bat Texas Leaguer could be a big deal if it happened at the right time. Then she was amazed at how the distance from home to first was such that a fast runner who hit a ground ball to the shortstop would be just *barely* out if the ball was fielded cleanly and thrown well. She was also surprised at how a fly ball had to be just *so* deep if the runner was to tag and make it home. My mom was into baseball.

My mom and I went to many Phillies games, less than a hundred, more than fifty. She was a great person to watch a game with because she was totally into the game and never needed anything, although she would get me whatever crap (hot dogs, caramel corn) I wanted. She didn't talk that much at the games, but when she noticed something, she mentioned it. It was always something interesting.

At home she listened to the games on the radio. She didn't like to watch them on television, but she would watch the tube if she had to. She hated it when they showed the view from behind the pitcher.

"That ruins it," she'd say.

I asked her why and she pointed out that you couldn't see the fielders' little moves, you couldn't see the base runners, and you couldn't see the pitcher's face.

But she listened to every Phillies game on the radio. I think she liked to picture the game in her mind.

Somewhere inside her, I knew there were pictures of Ireland. But my mom, like my dad, almost never talked to me about it. The only story she ever shared with me about her childhood in Ballyhaunis was the story of her First Holy Communion. And it was the only story she ever told me that made her visibly sad. It always made me feel that way also. It still does.

First Holy Communion is a huge day in an Irish Catholic kid's life. It's like ten birthdays rolled into one. In actuality, my mom's First Holy Communion was probably a happy day. For a kid in County Mayo, it had to be a highlight. At the beginning of the story I could see that the mere memory of the day was exciting to her. My mom's voice didn't go up and down. It was a steady, unending stream. But I could tell from the details that that was a big day.

When she told me about that big day in Ireland, I had already experienced my own First Holy Communion in New Jersey. It was not a jump-up-and-down day for me. It was nothing like Christmas. The best thing about it, I remembered, was that it took place at the end of May, and school was almost finished for a year. But I could tell that it had been a big, big deal to her. She remembered all of the details.

Half of the stuff she told me, I didn't understand. There was a lot of Irish stuff and church stuff that went right over my head. With my mom everything went by very fast. I didn't ask for clarification. There was, however, one detail that, to her, was horrible. It caused her, even fifty years later, enormous emotional pain. *The black shoes.*

When she got to the shoes, she paused, and she never paused. She swallowed or something. Then she went on. The river flowed on, just like usual. But then she repeated the thing. The detail. The shoes. The words stopped.

I was amazed. My mom was crying. Very quietly.

She recovered almost immediately and went on. But my attention was focused on the thing that made her stop instead of the rest of the story. It seemed to me a very small thing that made my mom cry, almost nothing at all really. The shoes? The sort of thing you forget quickly. She didn't forget quickly. Her parents, she told me, refused to buy her white shoes for the big day. The white shoes cost too much money, and First Holy Communion, while a big thing and a sacred day in Ireland, is only one day. They decided against the white shoes. That's a lot to spend for one day, Anne, they told her. Think of how much food you can buy with a pound, Annie. Think of that. So we can't get the shoes, Anne. Sorry, Anne. No white shoes.

"So we can't get the shoes, Anne. You'll get over it." That's what they told her, and that sentence burned its way into my heart. When she told me the story of the First Holy Communion and the black shoes in our kitchen in New Jersey, I could still feel how much those words had hurt her.

"So we can't get the shoes, Anne."

She said it again and looked out the window. Her face was set, accepting the way things go. But I could see that she was thinking back to the day she had heard the words. And her eyes showed that she had never really forgotten how much that hurt, how much it crushed her.

She looked out the window for a minute. Then she dabbed her eyes with a dishtowel, and she went back to whatever else there was.

I try to picture that scene. My mom had to receive her first communion with the "wrong shoes." First Holy Communion was held in the village church, the most important place in town, and Mom was there, wearing the same white dress her mother had worn, but she had to be in a long line of little girls in white dresses, the only one without white shoes. The only one with big ugly black shoes.

"I had to wear big ugly black shoes with laces." She put it that way, "Big ugly black shoes with laces." That was the part of the story that crushed her. She told me this story only once or twice. She couldn't get through it without crying at the memory of that distant humiliation.

I really don't believe she told anybody except my brother and sister and me the story. To be honest, I find that I cannot tell it now without feeling empty and bleak and very, very sad.

That was the one single major image I had of my mom's childhood—the black, ugly shoes and First Holy Communion, so I had, in my mind's eye, always imagined Ballyhaunis as a place of desperate poverty, a place where saving a pound was worth hurting a little girl. But when we drove into the little town of Ballyhaunis, I was quite stunned by what I saw on the way in. Ballyhaunis was doing very well. There were handsome homes and BMWs and handsomer, half-built homes and Mercedes Benzes and Jaguars and manicured lawns. Automatic sprinklers and cell phones and winding drives and high-school kids in convertible Beemers and smiling well-dressed people with really good haircuts.

No one seemed to be having difficulty coming up with the dough for the white shoes around there, the suburbs around the town.

The town itself looked exactly like every other little Irish town. Two banks, two pharmacies, an off-track betting place, three or four B&Bs, and a few pubs. Every place, of course, had a freshly painted sign.

Ballyhaunis was the first town I saw in Ireland with the names from my family tree on signs. Forde and Turley owned a lot of stuff here. Forde and Turley were doing well. We decided to stay at a B&B right in the town. The first one we saw was called The Avondale. It was a beautiful old place run by a very nice lady named Bridie Levins. I talked with her for a few moments and discovered that she not only knew my mom's family, she was actually related to me. Her uncle was my mom's cousin. I was going to say, "That means that you are my . . ." but I stopped myself because I knew that I could never finish the sentence until I drew one of those little family-tree charts and stared at it for about an hour and a half. Then I would be able to say, "You are my second cousin, once-removed," or something.

Bridie Levins told us that there was a pub named the Hazel, which was run by a Margaret Hopkins. Margaret Hopkins was Jimmy Hopkins's daughter, and Jimmy Hopkins, I had learned, was very close to the Forde girls. I had thought that this would be a major mystery, but once I got to Ballyhaunis, it wasn't.

Bridie said that my mom and her sisters liked to laugh a lot when they were young. That was not a big surprise. They liked dances. I remembered seeing an old yellow picture of my mom all dressed up in what looked like one of the *Untouchables* speakeasy scenes. In the picture she's laughing and her arm is around some guy who looks like the young Victor Mature. My mom must have had a few laughs hanging around with the young Victor Mature.

That night we went to the Hazel, which is a very nice pub: polished brass and dark wood and beautiful old pictures on the wallpapered walls. We found seats and asked for Margaret Hopkins. She came over right away. Margaret Hopkins was a very attractive woman in her forties. She was extremely open and gracious and talking to her was as easy as breathing.

She told us that yes, indeed, she knew my mom's sisters very well because they actually were, for a time, her baby-sitters. I tried to picture that. She didn't remember my mom much, but she had vivid memories of my mom's two sisters, Delia and Mary.

"Mary had that Yank accent," she said.

Margaret Hopkins told us about the sisters, who never married, living out there in the little house. They farmed a little. They didn't go out much, but when they did, they really liked to get dressed up. She also told us something totally surprising: My mother had a sister I had never heard of. She was never mentioned in any kind of family thing, and I had never heard a single word spoken about her.

She had been born with severe birth defects. My mom's sister could never walk. She had to be cared for all her life, and she died young, and she was not afterward discussed.

It amazed me, for a moment, that no one had ever mentioned my mom's sister. How could a detail that large go unmentioned for all those years? Wouldn't my mom, a woman of a thousand words, have referred to this sister at least once? (I asked my brother and my sister. To the best of their knowledge, my mom never said a single word about this sister.) I was amazed again at how some Irish people avoid talking about something they aren't comfortable with. They avoid it for lifetimes. My mom, who had said probably a million words in my presence, had never *mentioned* this sister.

The horror of life, the shared tragedy that all Irish people in some way share, this is a *given*. The nightmare is not a surprise; the absence of the nightmare is. If you are lucky enough to avoid the nightmares, above all, do not talk about them. Talking about them, even *mentioning* them, only encourages them. So any crippling, horrible malady is not to be talked about. Do you want it to approach?

In talking with the people in Ireland, I always knew, after a while, which subjects were *verboten*. There was always a look that told me. Sometimes a silence would fall and someone would say, in a low voice, "There's no luck in that."

Or just, "Not that."

I had been told this, sometimes in code, many times when I was in Ireland. "If you talk about bad things," I was told by a little man in a pub near Spanish Point, "the bad things hear their name, and they come because they've been called. Like a dog. So you never mention anything really horrible. If you get drunk or something and just mention them, they come.

They hear their name and they come. And you don't want that," he added emphatically.

The man from Spanish Point who said that was not smiling. He was very drunk, but I believe that he thought that he was speaking nothing but the truth, and I think, in a way, he was. In American baseball you do not mention it when somebody is pitching a no-hitter. In Ireland, you do not talk about the "bad things."

So my mom's sister, my aunt, my crippled aunt, was never mentioned.

We made an arrangement to talk with Jimmy Hopkins at eight the next night. Jimmy knew the sisters Forde very well. After all those years, I was going to go back to where everything began for my mother.

That night I tried to picture it as I fell asleep. I was now going to see the place that had always seemed like a place in a strange old fairy tale. The little house out in the woods. The house where they didn't buy the little girl the white shoes. The place where they broke the little girl's heart, a place like Hansel and Gretel's house. I was going to visit a place that had occupied a little place in my mind since I was a kid. But now it would have walls and a door and floors and windows. And real ghosts: little girls who fall asleep sobbing as they gaze through the dim light at the ugly black shoes on the floor next to the bed.

We arrived at the house at the appointed time. A little girl, maybe Jimmy's daughter, went with us as a sort of guide. It was very windy, but as clear as it gets in Ireland. It felt a little spooky walking out to find the house. I don't know why, but I felt extremely nervous and tight. My mouth was very dry.

My mom's house was about as big as our garage in our old house back in New Jersey. It was a tiny house, but much larger and nicer than my dad's place outside Athlone. It was white and yellow and the door was brown. It wasn't hard to see that, at one time, this had been a very nice little house. The little girl opened the door and I walked inside. I thought of Anne Forde as a little girl.

No one had been in the house for a long time. There were piles of cardboard and dirt and little metal parts that used to hold shelves and half-collapsed tables and strange wild plants growing up through the holes in the floor. There was so much of this overgrowth that it was difficult to walk. I shuffled along through the refuse, trying as well as I could to move from room to room. There seemed to be four rooms in the house, but it was hard to tell where one room ended and another began because there was so much stuff on the floor. I couldn't see the actual floor for the weeds and the junk.

I moved into a room that at one time must have been the kitchen. There was a big pile of shelves that had collapsed. I saw something shiny underneath them and I bent and grabbed the end of the shelf. I moved it back and saw that there were several shiny things under there but they were covered with dirt and pieces of something that seemed to be sheetrock and I shifted that over to the other side and I saw that there was another little stack of something, some square things with metal edges. I moved the sheetrock and saw that there was a pile of stuff that looked like a stack of pictures in cheap metal frames.

So I got the pile of metal frames in my hand and pulled them out from underneath. I nicked my finger doing this and it started bleeding. I ignored the blood from my finger, and I got the stack out and held it in my hands.

There on top, covered with dirt, there was something, a picture. So I brushed the dirt off and pulled it out and held it up and took my sleeve and wiped it off and I saw what it was.

What it was shocked me. It was me, a picture of me. During the disco era, smiling a stupid-looking grin. I had big, thick, grotesque sideburns. I had forgotten just how bad they looked. Now, three thousand miles from America, I was reminded. I tried to figure out just where I had been when that unfortunate picture was taken. Where was I? Some wedding in New Jersey? Yes, that was it. I couldn't remember who got married, but I remembered the wedding. Who took it? My sister. What was it doing here?

My mom had it enlarged and then sent it to her sister. A long time ago. Back when I was "stayin' alive."

Now, many years later, I stood there with the picture of me with the shirt with the widest collar in America in my mom's half-fallen-apart house in Loganboy. I looked at the picture and I thought about my mom and her handicapped sister and the three Forde girls, and getting on the boat, and coming back with a Yank accent, and how brief and strange human life can be.

I thought about that out in this house in the middle of a field in County Mayo, Ireland, and that made a chill run up my back.

I try to think of my mom's childhood. About Anne Forde and her sisters living in that little house and trying to make a living off the little land they farmed. And the one sister they never talked about. Someone would always have to be taking care of her. And my mom would be thinking of the future and its two choices. Go to America or become a nun. If she had become a nun of course I wouldn't even be here. Something happened to stop her every time. She thought that it was God stopping her. Maybe it was. She was absolutely certain that God decided what would happen in her life. For a long time, she thought that God was going to make my life very short. He didn't have that in mind. But when my mom got cancer and died she was absolutely certain that God decided it all, and she never questioned his judgment. She had sixty-plus years here and that was enough.

The last time I saw her alive, I told her how people often recover from cancer. She looked at me and said, "My life is over." She smiled.

⌒ *Coda* ⌒

We have done all right in the land of opportunity. Most of us have nice houses. My cousin Billy has a hotel with a pool on the roof. I have a cousin who is a lawyer (doesn't everybody). I also have a cousin who is a priest. If I were a priest, my mom would be happier with me, but if she's looking down at me she can see that I'm not doing anything seriously wrong. My dad is probably happy that I have a job. I can hear him say, "Considering what you have for brains it could be worse."

We've had a few tragedies. One cousin's son got heavily involved in drugs and spent some time in prison. I have a nephew who attempted suicide. I love him very much.

I have another nephew who became a big-shot in the motion picture business. Once I called him and his secretary told me he "was between his office and his car." If my mom were around she might refer to him as "Lord Muck from Shit Hill." I love him too.

A lot of the Irish blood is diluted. I married a girl whose dad is from France. As far as I know, only one of the first generation married an Irish girl. We are just about melted into the melting pot. My son doesn't even like U2; he prefers someone named Andrew W. Kay. His music sounds like a car accident to me. Jesus, Mary, and Joseph.

I guess I'm an American. But I think a lot about the little house in Mayo and the little house near Athlone. I know where I came from now, and I'm not forgetting until six of my friends are carrying me out to a big black car.

I went over to Ireland looking for my roots. I found them, but I also found something else. It sounds strange, but I'll say it: In Ireland I found God. When I got back to America, which is the only place that I can ever really call "home," I found that He came with me. How can I say something like that? How can I rationalize that one? The truth is, I can't. If I sound crazy to you, I understand. It sounds crazy to me too.

All I know is, things are permanently different now, and that is what the Old Country did to me. I don't feel the ground I'm walking on is all I'm going to experience anymore. I think that I've taken a number from the rack, and I'm waiting for it to be called. But I'm not tense about it. I'm calm. Let me amuse myself until it's my time. Maybe I'll do a crossword puzzle or raise children or write books. Let them call it when it's time. I felt like that in Ireland—as if someone were in the next room waiting for me—and the feeling came with me when I returned to America. I had never felt this way before, but I do now. I feel like there is somebody waiting for me. I don't go around screaming it. I don't knock on doors and tell people, but I feel it just the same. Maybe it's a delusion, but if it is, it's a darling illusion. It's a brilliant illusion; it is . . . if you want to feel this way, maybe you will. The plane is ready. Bring warm clothes. Good luck.

28 DATE DUE *DAYS*

JUL 2 6 2003		
AUG 2 6 2003		
SEP 0 9 2003		
SEP 2 3 2003		
OCT 0 7 2003		
OCT 2 1 2003		
NOV 2 9 2003		
2 6 2004		
MAR 1 8 2004		
	WITHDRAWN	
GAYLORD		PRINTED IN U.S.A.